Self-Analysis for the Psychotherapist

Self-Analysis for the Psychotherapist

The Moss Method

Aaron A. Moss

Writer's Showcase
San Jose New York Lincoln Shanghai

Self-Analysis for the Psychotherapist
The Moss Method

Writer's Showcase
an imprint of iUniverse.com, Inc.

For information address:
iUniverse.com, Inc.
5220 S 16th, Ste. 200
Lincoln, NE 68512
www.iuniverse.com

ISBN: 0-595-18588-6

Printed in the United States of America

Dedicated to Ruthie Stienman,
my ongoing encouragement and inspiration.

ACKNOWLEDGEMENTS

I am grateful to Theodore Jacobs, M.D. and Herbert S. Strean, D.S.W. for reviewing my manuscript and for their encouragement to proceed with the publication of the book. I also want to thank Sheldon Silberstein for editorial assistance and Sonya Ostrum for proofreading my manuscript.

PREFACE

In researching the literature, I found that in the last twelve years there has been a burgeoning of over 1,500 articles by analysts around the world dealing with countertransference (CTR). Within this group there were 158 articles that discussed the importance of self-analysis as a means of dealing with CTR. Gerhard Siebert, the famous German psychoanalyst, states the following: "acting out by the analyst in countertransference is unavoidable and initially occurs beyond the analyst's control..., by means of self-analysis the analyst's acting out in CTR can be therapeutically useful for working-out patient's problems."[1]

But there is another reason for doing self-analysis, which I consider even more important than improving your professional skill. Self-analysis can be a significant means of dealing with your own unresolved conflicts. Is there anyone who is free of conflicts and physical symptoms and/or personality problems related to these conflicts? Jaques Lacan, the renowned French psychoanalyst, believes that "only through death can we resolve our conflicts..., the various problems that get so much attention from psychoanalysts are not suffered exclusively by just a few

---

1 Siebert, Gerhard; *Forum for Psychoanalytic Review*; 1996; Vol. 12; 315—327.

people, but by all of us. There is no human being who is not either neurotic, psychotic or perverse."[2]

At a spring 1998 meeting of the Society of The New York School for Psychoanalytic Psychotherapy and Psychoanalysis, attended by about 150 psychoanalysts, Theodore Jacobs, MD, discussed in great detail a case history in which his own self-analysis enabled him to successfully 'work through' what would have been a dead-end impasse. Urging those present at the meeting to pursue ongoing self-analysis, he said, "...by tuning in on ourselves, gaining awareness of our experiences in sessions, *and grappling once again with the ghosts that haunt each of us,* [emphasis mine] we discover not only forgotten aspects of our selves but the inner world of our patients as well."[3]

Based on interviews with sixty four highly experienced practitioners, Carl Goldberg found that "self-analysis was believed by these practitioners to be indispensable, but poorly understood and underutilized."[4] There is no doubt in my mind that the reason for under-utilization of self-analysis is that no one has come forth with a technique for doing self-analysis. Those who have written about self-analysis rely on the concept of 'working through.' Each therapist has his own special method of doing this. At the meeting mentioned above, Theodore Jacobs stated, "...working through occurs *outside the office* when one might muse and reflect on events with a patient, on walks, in the car, taking a shower, fixing dinner, or while repairing something in his/her basement...At other times it operates while we sleep,

---

2   Jaques Lacan; *Lacan for Beginners*; Writers and Readers Publishing Inc.; New York, 1997, p. 94.

3   Jacobs, Theodore, MD; Seminar, March 8, 1998.

4   Goldberg, Carl; Yeshiva Univ., Albert Einstein Col. of Medicine, NY,: *The Unexplored in Self-analysis*; Psychotherapy; 1993 Vol. 30, 159-161.

giving rise to dreams that help to illustrate the conflicts stirred within us."[5] This method works well for Dr. Jacobs-and probably for many others. Nevertheless, there is no systematic method or technique for dealing with the associations and reflections that arise during the *'outside the office'* occurrences.

Alain Fine, a noted French psychoanalyst, says, "...a psychoanalyst's self-analysis is an indispensable parameter of experiences outside the analytic session..., the necessity of self-analysis for the psychoanalyst's satisfactory psychic and analytic functioning is a necessity..."[6]

Jacques Cain, another well-known French analyst, in discussing the need of the analyst to improve his/her potential in helping the patient, admonishes the therapist with, "...you must strive to carry out a state of continuous development, *which only stops at their death.* [emphasis mine]"[7]

Karen Horney, in her book, *Self-Analysis* published over fifty years ago stated:

> Granted that a considerable number of people can benefit from analytic therapy, but will they ever complete the work? Will there not always be problems left that are not solved or even touched upon? My answer is that there is no such thing as a complete analysis. This answer is not given in a spirit of resignation. Certainly, the greater the degree of self-transparency, the more freedom we can obtain, the better for us,...but the idea of a finished human product appears not only presumptuous,

---

5 Ibid
6 Fine, Alain; *The Analyst's Self-analysis: Some Questions and Reflections*; Revue-Francaise-de-Psychanalyse; 1990 Sep.-Oct., Vol. 54(5) 1221-1236.
7 Cain, Jacques; *The Psychoanalyst in Continuous Development*; JN: Revue Francaise de-Psychanalyse; 1992 Apr-Jun Vol. 56(2) 335-343.

but even, in my opinion, lacks any strong appeal...Life is a struggle; if when successful this struggle results in development and growth...continuous, ongoing self-analysis is one of the means that can help.[8]

Although there is general agreement among authorities that self-analysis should be an ongoing process, I have not found a single article in my research describing a method, a systematic technique or any kind of a procedure for doing self-analysis. I believe that my book is the first breakthrough. I have no doubt that others will follow when its feasibility will be accepted.

I started doing self-analysis about fifty years ago, when I was in my late thirties. I was still a practicing dentist. It is hard to believe that I, a lay person to the psychotherapy profession, was grappling with a procedure that to this very day is a challenge to the practicing psychoanalyst. I already had completed three years of analytic treatment with one analyst. Then, after a period of two years, I had two more years with another analyst. Both were of the orthodox Freudian school. Although I was discharged by both analysts, my stomach continued to be tense with anxiety. During that seven year period, I did extensive reading about psychoanalysis. With this background only, I started doing self-analysis.

Since I had never heard of anyone doing this, I was not sure whether what I was doing, self-analysis without a therapist, was feasible. Nevertheless, I continued because at the end of each session I always felt more relaxed. The physical and mental relaxation was akin to that of taking a tranquilizer. That was enough to motivate me to continue. But I was uncertain whether feeling better was attributable to my self-therapy or perhaps to autosuggestion in the style of the once popular Emile Coué, whose followers chanted the phrase, "Every day in every way I

---

8 See ref #3.

am getting better and better."[9] Or perhaps it was positive thinking, advocated by the Rev. Norman Vincent Peale, popular at the time, which in essence is also autosuggestion.[10]

Then, in the early 1950s, after several years of practicing my own brand of do-it-yourself analysis, I encountered a book by Karen Horney.[11] [12] What a thrill I experienced to discover that what I had been doing had been validated by this outstanding pioneer. Whatever doubts I had were forever dispelled. Thus, my book is the culmination of three important factors: 1) many thousands of hours of self-analysis; 2) my training as an analyst; and 3) experience with psychotherapists and patients, in my own practice of psychoanalysis.

Dr. Horney's motive for writing her book was to establish the validity and feasibility of self-analysis. Though she did not describe any practical procedures, she convinced me and others,

---

9 Brooks, Cyrus; *Emile Coué*; Dodd Mead; 1922.

10 Peale, Norman V.; *The Power of Positive Thinking*; Prentice Hall; NY, NY. 1952.

11 Horney, Dr. Karen; *Self Analysis*; W.W. Norton, NY, NY; 1943.

12 Dr. Horney was a prominent psychoanalyst in the 1940s and 50s. She was one of the early neo-Freudians who pioneered the breakaway from orthodox Freudian philosophy and practice. She was born in Hamburg, Germany in 1885, studied at the Berlin University and received her medical degree in 1913. She taught in the Berlin Psychoanalytical Institute, 1914—18. She participated in many congresses, among them the Historic Discussion of Lay Analysis chaired by Sigmund Freud. Dr. Horney came to The United States in 1932 and for two years she was the associate editor at The Psychoanalytic Institute, Chicago. In 1934 she came to New York and became a member to the teaching staff of the New York Psychoanalytic Institute until 1941. She was one of the founders of the New Association for the Advancement of Psychoanalysis and The American Institute for Psychoanalysis.

including many of her contemporary colleagues, that the rationale underlying the modality of self-analysis is valid and applicable. She claimed that at times even a lay person can learn self-analysis. Unfortunately, Dr. Horney's book was intended as a purely theoretical presentation. Therefore, it did not include any practical procedures that one might follow. In contrast, my book deals with the practical aspects of a do-it-yourself technique. I devised a six-step procedure that I named the Moss Method for Self-analysis. My book is intended as a guide for the practicing psychoanalyst.

One of the main reasons that self-analysis never caught on in the profession is the belief that it does not work. The fact that Freud terminated his self-analysis after publishing the case of Irma Dream, had a profound effect on his followers.[13] Karen Horney's book was the first to take issue with the disbelievers. Her conviction of the validity of self-analysis was based on the experience with her own self-analysis and those of some of her colleagues and their patients. The main objection of the disbelievers is that a person can not be objective enough to see and feel the whole of one's self. I agree that the help of a therapist is more efficient. Nevertheless, although a dental prosthesis may not be as efficient as one's own teeth, a denture enables a person to eat and an artificial leg enables a person to walk. So too, if you apply the innovative procedures of the Moss Method, you will find that self-analysis is feasible and workable. The Moss Method is very specific in what to look for and in how to do it. I characterize this as the WHAT and the HOW. This innovation overcomes much of the subjectivity which heretofore has been an obstacle to self-analysis.

---

13 Blum, Harold; *The Irma Dream, Self-analysis, and Self-Supervision*; Journal of the American Psychoanalytic Association; 1996 Vol. 44, 511-532.

The Moss Method, a six-step procedure, is based on a number of concepts and principles pertinent to the practical procedures for self-analysis. You may be familiar with some of the theoretical ideas and concepts, while others will be unfamiliar to you because they are ideas and devices of my own invention. As yet, they do not appear in the literature.

This book has two sections: section one deals with the basic theoretical concepts upon which the practical procedures of the Moss Method are built. Section one must be thoroughly understood and kept in the forefront of your mind when carrying out the practical procedures. Section two deals with the practical details of the six-step procedures. The book has a glossary that includes terms and definitions, some of which are of my own invention and therefore are not found in the literature.

CONTENTS

ACKNOWLEDGEMENTS vii

PREFACE ix

Section One: (Theoretical) 1

    CHAPTER 1: MIND SET 3

    CHAPTER 2: THE MAGICAL POWER

             OF THE UNCONSCIOUS 13

    CHAPTER 3: HUMANIZATION OF THE BEAST 23

    CHAPTER 4: KEEP THE SHOW ON THE ROAD 29

    CHAPTER 5: NATURE'S OBSESSION WITH SEX 38

    CHAPTER 6: WE ARE ALL HYPNOTIC SUBJECTS . . .49

    CHAPTER 7: SYMBOLISM: THE LANGUAGE

             OF THE UNCONCIOUS 58

    CHAPTER 8: FANTASY CONSTELLATION 64

    CHAPTER 9: THE AGP SYNDROME 70

Section two: (Practical) 83

    CHAPTER 10: THE DREAM: Part 1 85

    CHAPTER 11: STEP I: The Dream: Part 2 96

CHAPTER 12: STEP II: THE LIST 102
CHAPTER 13: STEPS III and IV: FREE ASSOCIATION 111
CHAPTER 14: STEP V: RECAPITULATION 120
CHAPTER 15: STEP VI: ANALYTIC
                     INTERPRETATION (Part One) 124
CHAPTER 16: STEP VII: ANALYTIC
                     INTERPRETAtION (Part Two) 131
GLOSSARY 149

Section One

(Theoretical)

CHAPTER 1

MIND SET

The title of this book may lead you to believe that it deals with how to improve your skill as a therapist. That most certainly will happen if you successfully incorporate into your life the Moss Method for Self-analysis. But the primary focus of this book is to help you to grow emotionally; to become more mature; to be healthy, free of any pathology; to be functioning at your maximum, creative potential. There is no doubt that if you pursue this goal, you will be a better therapist.

Starting therapy with a new patient, you, the analyst, must explain the analytic procedure including discipline, honesty, free association, the nature and character of resistance and how it is manifested. (Naturally, you use your judgment regarding the timing of the foregoing.) What you must do is establish the proper mind set. Since with self-analysis you are both the patient and the analyst, it is imperative for you, the patient, to have the proper mind set to be successful with the Moss Method for Self-analysis. The foregoing is precisely what this chapter attempts to do.

The correct mind set involves motivating you to make emotional growth and maturity the MOST IMPORTANT GOAL OF YOUR LIFE. Although everyone will agree to that, what this necessitates is beyond the will and capacity of many individuals. There are times that you may have to endure so much unbearable emotional pain and wrenching conflict that is so unbearable that you settle for the status quo and live in a state of denial. As psychoanalysts, you are well aware that what is concealed in your patient's unconscious is there because it is impossible for your patient to cope with what was repressed. You and I have exactly the same problem.

Examples of such painful emotions and conflicts are the following: putting your objecting parent in a nursing home; needing to move to a different part of the country for health reasons; changing jobs; feeling oppressive guilt of a sexual nature; guilt for believing you are a failure as a parent whose child is a hopeless drug addict; having an accident while driving that leaves your wife a paraplegic; recalling horrible memories, such as being raped; seeing your buddy's body torn wide open on the battlefield during war; ending a bad relationship which is masochistic self-destructive and beyond salvation; failing to terminate analytic treatment of a patient either for your personal aggrandizement or your inability to accept the fact that you have failed.—The latter may be a bitter pill to swallow. You will rationalize reasons to continue treatment. It is not uncommon for psychotherapists to feel like frauds.—The list could be almost endless.

What follows is a description of an actual case that serves as an example of the foregoing: Patient X, a man in his middle sixties, was locked in a bad marriage. His marriage was motivated by his guilt. Twenty-seven years earlier, he told his girl friend that he must discontinue seeing her because their sexual intimacy had gotten out of hand. He tried to explain to her that he was not ready for marriage. She broke down in an uncontrollable fit of crying. For several days he was obsessed with unbearable guilt. The torment was instantly relieved when he proposed marriage to her. They eloped and were married a week later. That was the genesis of a twenty-seven year marriage. He was convinced that the relationship was emotionally destructive to both himself and his spouse, yet he was incapable of change. He made several attempts to break the marriage starting with the first year, but each time he could not cope with the crushing guilt of abandoning his spouse. The relationship was characterized by mutual hostility, constant arguments, sexual failure that made him seek extramarital sex, secrecy, anxiety, and a very low self-esteem for his infidelity, his weakness and his cowardice. He was convinced that it was his lack of emotional strength that was the reason he remained fixed in what he called "a marital trap." His conflict was so tormenting that for periods of months, and sometimes years, he repressed the conflict. During these periods he lived in a state of denial. His rationalization was that his marriage was not so bad and that it would last "till death do us part." But periodically during all those years the conflict would again emerge.

My colleagues, all the above is a disclosure of my own marital experience. Right from the outset of my marriage I realized that it was a mistake. I stayed married for twenty-seven years. I was emotionally incapable of making the change. During all those years my professional success was spectacular even though my emotional life was tumultuous with agonizing emotional distress. My conflict took a toll on my body. I leaned heavily on alcohol, tranquilizing drugs and sleeping pills. I developed psychosomatic symptoms including stomach and heart problems and sexual impotency. Ten years of psychoanalysis that started after the second year of my marriage was futile. I then resumed my own therapy of daily self-analysis. I used a procedure that I devised by myself.

I discovered that self-analysis gave me relief from my emotionally disturbed state and my taut, nagging stomach. I then proceeded with daily sessions of self-analysis. My motive was not to break my marriage but only to alleviate the emotional distress and the toll it was taking on my body. But my marital situation almost always emerged during my sessions. There were periods of months that I neglected my sessions. During those periods I was in a state of denial of my marital conflict. I believed my marriage would be forever. But when other aspects of my life—my health, hysterical anxiety, neurasthenia, etc.—became oppressive, I resumed my regular daily sessions. But the repressed marital conflict always emerged as the root of all my problems. With the passing of time, and by means of systematic self-analysis, I made strides in emotional growth. I grew strong enough to terminate the marriage. This was a spin-off of my growth and maturation. But for almost an entire year after the end of my marriage, I experienced agonizing guilt. I had fantasies that I was a parent abandoning my dependent child. Several times during that first year, I actually picked up the phone to call my ex-wife to beg forgiveness and to resume our twenty-seven year relationship. That would give me instant relief, the same as when I married her out of guilt. But now, in contrast to caving in as on several previous attempts, I was now strong enough to hold my grounds. Although my guilt never left me, as time passed, I continued with my emotional growth, so that today I am totally free of guilt. I finally broke the umbilical cord and made a complete separation from my mother!

I made systematic self-analysis a part of my daily routine when I discovered that it not only relieved my emotional and psychosomatic symptoms, but also helped me to detach myself from my fixated, traumatic past and resume emotional growth. With that discovery, I had relinquished my need for neurotic symptoms. Once I made the important discovery of the connection between systematic self-analysis and emotional growth, I made growth and maturity the most important goal of my life. Thus, my systematic self-analysis was motivated by this goal and *not* by the breaking of my marriage. But my marriage became an obstacle that thwarted my goal of continuous growth.(All unresolved critical conflicts are obstacles to growth.) With this insight, plus the sizeable emotional growth that occurred over the years, I developed the ego strength to terminate my marriage, to resume growth, and to achieve the most important goal of my life, PERPETUAL GROWTH. Approaching my ninetieth birthday, I feel that I am still growing.

There is a twofold purpose for my foregoing disclosure. The first is to indicate the nature of the kind of conflicts that one may experience. The worse thing you can do when confronted with a critical conflict *of any nature* is to repress it. In so doing, you live in a state of denial. This will not only stunt your growth process, but it will reverse it and result in untoward consequences, including personality aberrations and illness. It is by far healthier to struggle with the conflict than to repress it.—Unfortunately, when the ego is weak, i.e., stunted in emotional growth, this can't be done. Successful self-analysis will strengthen the ego— The insidious aspect of repression and denial is that you never connect all the resulting consequences with the repressed conflict. Only by means of psychoanalysis do you make that connection. The second is to serve as a model to those colleagues who may identify their own conflict with the above disclosure. I have had two colleagues as patients with serious marital conflict in addition to other problems. In one individual, a woman, the analysis was a success. The spin-off was termination of her fifteen year old marriage. The other, a man married for twenty-three years, had to quit therapy because he developed acute gastric pain whenever the analysis focused on his marriage. He perceived the end result of the analysis would be to terminate his marriage. The irony of this case was that he, himself, was extremely critical of his spouse and of his marriage He is now living in a state of denial, with an illness diagnosed as cancer.

The foregoing is an attempt to demonstrate how important it is to make emotional growth and maturity the most important goal of one's life. This will happen only by total commitment to that goal. The latter necessitates the capacity and the willingness to endure the pain of self-confrontation, your patient must. Therefore, your resistance to self-analysis is no less than that of your patient. However, there will be no one to prompt you, to urge you, to encourage you or to consult. It all must be generated by a powerful will and commitment to make emotional growth and maturity the number one goal of your life. To achieve that goal, if you must commit yourself to pay whatever the price is in inconvenience, discomfort and suffering, you will be able to endure the pain. Successful self-analysis will strengthen your ego to make the necessary changes in your life. The Moss Method demands a powerful will and determination to succeed. It must be carried out daily and systematically. Think of me as an athletic coach giving a pep talk to his/her team before the start of the game in order to build a fighting spirit. That is the intent of this chapter.

Ideally, you must have a session with yourself every day in the week. The time required for a session is approximately one hour.[1] When I mentioned this to a colleague, he replied, "I'd have to get up four o'clock in the morning."

"If that were necessary," I told him, "I would still recommend it. But you don't have to."

---

1   A detailed breakdown of the time required for each step is presented in the epilogue.

"What do you mean?" he asked me.

"Your first appointment of the day should be with yourself."

"But that would upset my whole day's schedule and would also cut into my income," he objected.

"Don't you consider yourself important enough for that?"

This short dialogue is presented to make you feel that you should be more important to yourself than are any of your patients. Unless you feel that way, you will not carry out the rigorous self-discipline demanded by the Moss Method. Your analytic sessions with yourself must take priority over everything else, except of course, eating, sleeping, your morning toilet routine, etc. But going to a theater, playing bridge, going to a sports event, playing tennis, reading a book, writing a letter, making phone calls and the like are activities that most of the time are not of critical importance. These are the kinds of reasons or rationalizations that are a manifestation of resistance. When you put off the analytic session with yourself, regardless of the reason, you must always suspect your unconscious resistance to be the real reason. Nobody puts a gun to your head to determine your options and behavior. (There will be much more said, later in the book, about how resistance is manifested.) When and how your sessions should occur will be discussed in great detail later in the book. What I am trying to do now is simply to establish the correct mind set to make the Moss Method a success. With this in mind, I admonish you to "keep your eye on the ball." And what is the ball?

The ball is maximum physical health and emotional maturity. Herbert Strean quotes Reuben Fine, a well known, prolific writer on psychoanalysis, regarding the goal, "…you must learn to love rather than to hate, have sexual gratification, a feeling for life that is guided by reason, have an adequate role in family, have a sense of identity, be creative, have a role in the social order, be able to communicate and be reasonably free of neurotic or psychiatric symptoms...[2]

You must step aside and take stock of yourself. If you think rationally, you will consider yourself just as important, or even more so, than your patients. Therefore, you should treat yourself accordingly. You will consider the appointment with yourself as the most important of the day. Feeling this way about yourself will enable you to make the changes in your life necessary for the fulfillment of your goal. If you do not perceive yourself in this light, you can always find excuses and rationalize why you don't have the time. Such a reason indicates the lack of will, determination and commitment necessary for the needed discipline. If this is the case, you must be honest with yourself. Either you have not made continuous growth the number one goal of your life, or you are resisting the pursuit of that goal.

A very important manifestation of resistance is the pessimistic belief that self-analysis is not feasible. To believe that it does not work and that your efforts are futile is a very common form of resistance. This belief may appear in your dreams, but in symbolic form. Like your patient who keeps appointments diligently, yet has great resistance to the analysis, so too, you, who may conscientiously follow the Moss Method, will have the same unconscious resistance as your patient. Just as with your patient, not every session will be successful. Success is measured in terms of months or years of treatment. For the beginner of the Moss Method, the first session in which insight is gained is a very powerful impetus. Self-analysis is a form of struggle that demands total commitment. It is impossible to gather up enough strength and energy needed to make self-analysis work when

---

2   Strean, Herbert S.; *Resolving Resistances in Psychotherapy*; Brunner/Mazel; 1990, p. 32.

feelings of doubt and futility exist. I cannot over emphasize this enough. You must not be influenced by those in the profession whose attempts at self-analysis have failed. Listen to those who are successful with self-analysis, such as Dr. Theodore Jacobs and others whom I quoted in the preface. The changes in my life are proof that the Moss Method works.

My conviction is that success as a therapist is a natural spin-off of successful self-analysis. The main goal of self-analysis should be to be free of all illness; to have a productive, creative mind; to be in a mature and continued state of emotional growth, on to old age when the physical body begins to deteriorate, one should experience a greater degree of emotional stability with a minimum of anxiety; have a satisfying sex life; and a good feeling about one's self and one's life while riding the crest of the wave of happiness and optimism for the future. Is any price too much to pay for this?

In the previous paragraph, I deliberately omitted the idea that one should strive for a life free of conflict. To rid yourself of many indoctrinated beliefs and values you acquired in the formative period of your life can not be done without greater conflict in ideas of sex, religion, righteousness, respect for authority (parents and government), political doctrines, revolution, family values, homophobia, feminism, death, etc. The list could go on and on. Don't retreat from conflict! Although repression of conflict usually will give short term relief, the long term effects are destructive. It reverses the growth process, denying all the benefits of a happy life. A healthy resolution of conflict often results in a springboard leap forward in growth and maturity. One of my prayers is: "Dear God, please don't spare me conflict; but give me the back strong enough to cope with it." God has heard my prayer and has granted my wish. At the end of the ninth decade of my life, I still have conflicts, but I am able to cope with them so that I still continue to grow. You, too, can accomplish the same if you "keep your eye on the ball."

CHAPTER 2

THE MAGICAL POWER
OF THE UNCONSCIOUS

One who is naive perceives the unconscious as irrational and chaotic.[3] By all normal standards of thinking, the unconscious is totally inconsistent with all rational thinking. The unconscious has magical powers. It can convert a mole hill into a high mountain. For example, a person may react to a summons to appear in court for a traffic violation as though it were a summons to be executed. Sounds crazy? It is. What the conscious mind, the intellect, perceives as magic is the tyical thought process of the unconscious. It is mystical and infantile. Opposing and contradictory

---

3 I refer to the unconscious mind as that area of the psyche which is not in the immediate field of awareness; its content may become known by means of analyzing dreams, fantasies, behavior, and/or neurotic symptoms. I use the term unconscious throughout this book to mean the unconscious mind. I exclude that part of the unconscious that deals with basic life functions such as respiration, cardiovascular digestion and glandular activity, even though I am fully aware that they are functions controlled by the unconscious mind.

thoughts, emotions, beliefs, desires, etc. exist side by side at one and the same time. These contradictory thoughts may intrude into your overt behavior and/or conscious thoughts and perceptions. How this is possible is precisely what perplexes the conscious mind, the intellect. Yet that is the characteristic way in which the unconscious functions. By intellectual standards, you can characterize the unconscious as 'crazy' and chaotic. But if you understand the dynamics of the unconscious, you will discover that there is rationale and order to what appears to be chaotic. Only by means of psychoanalysis can you discover this. I shall now describe pertinent aspects of the unconscious mind.

One may view the size of the conscious mind relative to the unconscious as the size of the earth compared to the size of the universe in which the earth is a tiny speck. Notwithstanding this, the conscious mind has the capacity to sort time and space that the unconscious mind totally lacks. This one aspect alone is of significant importance in one's attempt to understand the unconscious mind. It lumps past, present, and future together as though all three exist simultaneously. One may dream about an event that may have occurred 25 years ago, or relive past traumas in one's dreams or fantasies as though they were actually occurring in the present. One lumps one's own image with that of persons other than oneself. In dreams, for instance, several different people may be the whole or parts of oneself. A child fantasizes itself to be a father, mother, baby sister or big brother, the policeman, teacher, one of the same or opposite sex, or one's good doll or bad doll, etc. Such identification is not only the characteristic of childhood fantasy, but such fantasies continue throughout one's life.

The unconscious does not mature with time as does the intellect. There is no such thing as a mature unconscious. The characteristics of an adult's unconscious is no different from that of a child, or even an infant. In adult fantasies you may identify your own self-image with several different roles simultaneously, in the same way the child does. For example, a mother of a three-year-old child may identify with the role of her own mother while simultaneously fantasizing herself to be her own child. When punishing your child, your unconscious perceives that you are your own mother punishing the 'badness' within yourself. (This phenomenon is called fantasy constellation which is discussed in Chapter 8.) Does it sound crazy? This actually is the bizarre way in which the unconscious functions. In the chapter that follows I shall cite case histories that illustrate the foregoing bizarre aspects of the unconscious mind.

Though the conscious mind, the intellect, is non-existent at birth, the unconscious mind is as functionally developed as it ever will be during one's entire life. The unconscious mind is a repository of every event, experience, thought and emotion dating back to the primordial past, including the memory of our primordial ancestors. How does one know this? It is the genius of both Jung and Freud, who have given humankind the key to explore, decipher and decode the symbolic language of the unconscious. One's conscious thoughts together with dreams, neurotic symptoms, slips, errors, mistakes, accumulated works of all the creative art forms, literature, folklore, anthropological studies, etc. compose a body of symbolic material which, when correlated and deciphered, can give, with certainty, the contents and nature of the unconscious mind by decoding the symbolism. One now has the key that opens up doors of the heretofore unknown vast universe of the unconscious. The most effective device of psychoanalysis for penetrating the unconscious mind is the phenomenon of free association. Without a thorough understanding and application of this phenomenon, the psychoanalytic modality is impossible. Because it is the foundation that lies at the base of the self-analytic technique, I discuss free association, in great detail in subsequent chapters.

An extremely important characteristic of the unconscious mind is the fact that it is always active, whether awake, asleep or unconscious under general anesthesia, or comatose. This activity starts before birth and ends with death. Notice the changing facial expression of a sleeping infant. One sees the fears, joys, and other deep emotions indicating the infant is dreaming. Although dreaming occurs at all ages from birth to death, the substance and contents of dreams are limited by one's age. Dreams of a two month old infant consist of intrauterine life, the trauma of birth and all experiences that occurred during the two month period since birth. An infant of six months of age may have all the dreams of a two-month old infant, plus additional dreams such as haven fallen off the highchair when it was four months old. An infant of one year may recall toilet training. At age three, there may be experiences of jealousy and hate involving sibling rivalry if there were a younger child. At age five, the first day in preschool, the child may have experienced panic at being separated from the parent and left alone in a strange and hostile environment. At age seven an injection of a local anesthetic by the dentist resulted in fighting and screaming. Thus, starting at birth, the number of experiences that one could dream about keep accumulating. Now consider an individual of age twenty, forty or sixty. The number of accumulated life experiences in a person of 60 years of age are vast, but still finite, as more experiences continue to occur.

Now, bearing in mind that the unconscious is timeless, any one or combination of experiences, regardless of the chronological order of their occurrence, can be intermixed alongside of any other experience or any combination of experiences as though any or all happened simultaneously in the past or are taking place in the present or will happen in the future. Any current overt reality may reactivate not only past experiences but even past fantasies stored in the unconscious mind. The reactivation may be provoked by similarity or association of even a fleeting, flimsy, irrelevant, unrelated, direct, or indirect or symbolic connection. As pointed out, a mother scolding a child may fantasize a dual role of simultaneously being her own mother and her own child, as though the clock were turned back a generation in time. Is this bizarre? Absolutely! Comprehending and applying this bizarre phenomenon is the basis of psychoanalysis.

What follows is a detailed discussion of hypnotic behavior for the purpose of demonstrating phenomena characteristic of human behavior. Under hypnosis, an individual can be regressed and thereby either recall or reenact past experiences entirely forgotten and beyond voluntary recall. During the many years I taught and practiced hypnosis, I regressed many dozens of subjects.[4][5] As a lecturer and instructor of numerous seminars on hypnosis, I would generally select one or more of the participants to demonstrate the various hypnotic phenomena. At a hypnosis seminar, consisting of about 35 participants (only physicians, dentists and psychologists were eligible to attend these seminars), I selected a male physician of about fifty years of age. Since he was a very good subject, I was able to regress him with ease. While under

---

4   In the late 1940s I was considered one of the pioneers who introduced hypnosis to the allied medical professions. Up to then hypnosis was in the gutter and was used only by vaudeville performers and by charlatans. I traveled around the country giving lectures and seminars to physicians, dentists and psychologists at meetings and in universities. My book, *Hypnodontics,* was the first book ever published that dealt with medical or dental use of hypnosis.

5   Moss. A. A., *Hypnodontics: Hypnosis in Dentistry;* Dental Items Pub. Co., N.Y., 1952.

hypnosis, I suggested to him that he was seeing, in his mind's eye, a clock with the hands going in the reverse direction.—A subject under hypnosis, can carry on a conversation with the hypnotist.—At first I suggested that the hands of the clock were moving slowly. They gradually picked up speed until they were spinning backwards in time. From a clock I switched to a calendar. Months and years were moving backwards rapidly. Occasionally, I elicited a response from the subject. At age twelve, the subject discontinued speaking English and started speaking in German. Fortunately, my familiarity with German made it possible for me to continue the conversational rapport. Time kept going backwards until he was about five years old. His language again changed into still another, which now I could not understand. A participant in the group, also a physician, volunteered with an explanation, "He is speaking in a German dialect, Dr. Moss."

"Do you understand this dialect?" I asked him. He did. I then used him as an interpreter thereby maintaining my rapport with the subject.

At the age of about three and a half, the subject started to struggle and tremble and went into a paroxysm of convulsive weeping. By means of the interpreter and without too much difficulty, I was able to grasp what was taking place. At age three and a half years, he fell off a slide located in a playground. He suffered lacerations and bleeding from his left arm and hand. He was then rushed to a hospital for treatment. To close the wounds, a number of sutures were required. All this was being reenacted (revivified) as though the past was actually occurring in the present. If I had rehearsed the event with a professional actor, I couldn't have been more effective in astounding the participants of the seminar. I then gave the subject a posthypnotic suggestion that upon wakening he would not recall anything of what happened while in the hypnotic trance state. My reason for inducing amnesia is that this deeply buried traumatic experience, which lay dormant in the unconscious, could easily become a currently reactivated trauma if brought back into consciousness without provisions for the therapeutic management of the recall of the forgotten experience.

After awakening the subject, I permitted the seminar participants to question him. Because of the posthypnotic amnesia, he hadn't the slightest memory or recollection either of what had happened under hypnosis, or of the trauma that occurred when he was three-and-a-half years old. The subject was then told what he revealed during the hypnotic state. He was truly surprised at what he was told. He reacted as though it hadn't happened to him but instead to some other person. His response was purely intellectual curiosity without personal, emotional involvement. There are thousands of similar experiences of regression described in the literature by me and others who have worked with experimental and clinical hypnosis.

I did not question or investigate the subject, a physician, to find out if he had any currently existing effects of that long forgotten trauma. It is possible that he may have had long shadows cast over his life resulting in aberrations such as phobias, character disorder, neurotic symptoms, etc. that may have originated from this trauma. There may have been aspects of this experience found in his dreams or fantasies. In my career as a dentist, I have uncovered many dental phobias that were the direct result of long- forgotten, traumatic childhood experiences.

The foregoing hypnotic experiment demonstrates a number of phenomena:
1) Whatever happens at any time in one's past is permanently stored into one's computer-like unconscious.
2) Under certain conditions, long past traumatic experiences can become re-activated.

3) There is no chronological perception of events or experiences because the unconscious is timeless.

4) Upon re-activation, past, present and future become interchangeable.

5) An individual may not have the slightest awareness or memory of past events and experiences even though such events may impact on one's perceptions and/or behavior.

There is a reciprocal involvement between the conscious and the unconscious. Often the determination of your reaction to a person you meet for the first time, positive or negative, is made by the unconscious. Unknowingly, you perceive something about that person that impacts on your unconscious. It may be his/her facial expression, hair, voice quality, eyes, nose, ears, shabby clothes, bulging abdomen, demeanor etc. that you associate with your spouse, father, mother, brother, sister, uncle, teacher, next door neighbor, policeman, etc. The irony of this association phenomenon is that you are totally oblivious of the unconscious involvement.

Every situation, event, or any kind of occurrence in your life, that is invested with an 'emotional charge' provokes an unconscious response. There are no exceptions to this rule. For example, if your employer disciplines you for some deed or misdeed, you respond, usually unknowingly, as you did when you were a child and were disciplined by your parent or your school teacher. Another example is someone getting a promotion that you feel you should have gotten, awakens a sibling rivalry response in which your mother discriminated against you by showing favoritism towards your brother or sister.

The always-active unconscious often associates some aspect of your reality with something in your unconscious. The effects of a childhood sexual abuse always impacts on one's adult sexual experiences. A woman who was raped will often encounter difficulties in her relationships with men. The unconscious never ceases its impact on our perceptions and behavior. (In Chapter 5, "We All Are Hypnotic Subjects," I will discuss how much of our perception and behavior originates from the unconscious, as though we are responding to a post hypnotic suggestion.) We find rational reasons for our perceptions and behavior, totally oblivious of the unconscious motivation.

An anecdote apropos of how our attitudes and state of mind is determined by our unconscious deals with an old begger-woman in the streets of New York. She was always cheerful and smiling. A passerby, handing her some money, but curious about her appearance of happiness asked her, "You seem to be a happy person in spite of your predicament. Are you really happy"?

"Oh yes, I am," she answered.

"To what do you attribute your happiness?"

"I am a fortunate woman. I have only two teeth, one on the upper jaw and one on the lower. Every day I thank God that they meet."

There are two concepts that this anecdote illustrates, pertinent to how the unconscious effects our state of mind. 1) Very often we find something in the outer environment and rationalize how we feel, oblivious of the fact that it is our unconscious that determines our feelings, perceptions and behavior,[6] 2) What is in the unconscious often simulates a posthypnotic suggestion. The woman in the above anecdote acted as though she were carrying out a posthypnotic suggestion to always be happy. Her rationalization was her two teeth that came together.

In the foregoing, I described a traumatic experience of an individual, three-and-a half years old, to indicate that whatever is in the unconscious is there forever. This also applies to your own

---

6   This concept will be referred to throughout this book.

childhood conditioning and cultural indoctrination regarding moral and ethical values. Samples of such indoctrination deal with religion, marriage, premarital sex, single mothers, homosexuality, racism and patriotism. The list can go on and on. If you consider yourself to be an atheist, but at some time in your past you were a believer, you still are a believer, in so far as your unconscious is concerned. Some of my patients who vehemently proclaimed their atheistic beliefs, were shocked when in the course of their analytic investigation, they discovered within themselves a strong belief in a deity. Likewise, if you ever believed that premarital sex is sinful, it remains sinful forever in your unconscious. If you were ever a racist, in your unconscious you still are a racist. This applies to all beliefs and prejudices you have ever had. You can NEVER eradicate what is now or what ever was in the concealed world of your unconscious. The significance of this is that you often have guilt or irrational feelings about something, but you can't explain why. When doing your self-analysis you will discover in your unconscious the reason for your irrational feelings.

The next chapter, "Humanization of the Beast," will deal with how our disciplinary conditioning in our early formative years affects our unconscious for the rest of our lives.

CHAPTER 3

HUMANIZATION OF THE BEAST

We are a species of the animal kingdom known as Homo Sapiens. What follows is a very brief discussion of how we become humanized. The process of humanization starts at birth. In our intrauterine existence we are no different from the other mammals emotionally, culturally, intellectually, etc. Then what determines our thoughts relative to lifestyle, attitudes, philosophy, behavior, and value-and-belief system as human beings? This chapter is an attempt to answer that question.

At birth the human animal, like the rest of the animal kingdom, has only one dominant instinct, namely, to survive. Without being helped to survive, the newborn, both human and non-human, would perish. Because parents, or parent substitutes, have the power of life and death over the infant, it perceives the parent a thousandfold more omnipotent than any God is perceived by the most fanatic, religious zealot—an existential concept.— Survival, the powerful survival power, demands and achieves humanization, i.e., adaptation to our culture.

A nonverbal communication between parent and child develops starting at birth. An infant less than three weeks old responds quite differently in an environment of tranquillity, love, and security compared to another in a neurotic environment of turbulence and hostility. Love and acceptance equates to security, while disapproval equates to rejection, which in turn translates to death or annihilation. Imagine a person with a pistol to your head, ready to fire the moment you disobey. This is how the totally dependent infant and/or young child must feel.

The attitudes of one's parents relative to the child's or infant's bodily functions, (defecating, urinating), eating, sleeping, making noises or other kinds of disturbances in the household, already have their marked effect on the infant long before it reaches the age of six months. By then the infant already has been conditioned to recognize approval or disapproval by the parents.[7] The infant and/or child is rewarded, punished, chastised and made to feel guilty, hundreds of times for reasons he/she at first finds incomprehensible. Adaptation through submission or adjustment is a necessity based on the survival instinct. The infant/child is gradually conditioned to learn what is acceptable and what is not. Just as Pavlov's dogs were conditioned, so, too, are we conditioned.[8]

SUBMISSION, CONFORMITY = LOVE AND ACCEPTANCE = SECURITY, SURVIVAL. In contrast DEFIANCE, REBELLION, RESISTANCE = GUILT, PUNISHMENT, REJECTION = INSECURITY, THREAT TO SURVIVAL, ANNIHILATION. What follows is an elaboration of these equations.

---

7 Spock, Dr. Benjamin; Commonsense Book of Child and Infant Care; 1944.
8 Pavlov, Ivan Petrovich; (1885-1931) A Russian physiologist, recognized as the leader of the school of conditioned reflex psychology. His laboratory experiments dealt with dogs.

The infant, on its way to becoming the growing child, must submit its own will and feelings to that of the parents. Acts of submission assuring survival. The young child not only willfully and consciously avoids forbidden, overt acts, but it involuntarily represses thoughts of forbidden acts from reaching consciousness. By the time you, the therapist, reached the age of five, you already had repressed not only the desire for forbidden acts but also many hundreds of forbidden thoughts. Thus, by the time you reached the tender age of five, you already had become a FUGITIVE FROM YOURSELF!

In the first grade in school, the child already has been so conditioned that any child different from the others becomes suspect. That suspect child is ostracized as being bad, evil or crazy and becomes the target of an abusive gang-up by all of its peers. We know how cruel children are when they single out, isolate and gang up against a child who is different. In adult life this takes on the practice of "Don't pay attention or listen to that one because he/she is crazy, a nut, an extremist, a communist, a foreigner, a Jew or a fascist." Once one is perceived as one of the former, such a person, is ridiculed, persecuted or ignored. Thus, society insulates itself from those of us who can influence others to feel or be that which our culture or environment prohibits, i.e., acting out the animal instincts. In short, we have been conditioned to be members of a herd in which others tend to do much of the thinking for us; tell us what is right or wrong; good or bad; moral or immoral, or righteous; what beliefs we should hold; what our goals in life should be; and what we should live or die for. We have no control over how these belief and value systems have been imposed on us.

In our Judeo-Christian culture, there are many conflicting forces in competition with each other for the capture and control of our minds. Which of these dominates a given individual depends to a large extent on the environment into which one is born. A person born into the Rockefeller family will have one set of values and beliefs. Another born into a family of generations of orthodox rabbis will have still another. What you become is the result of the sum total of all those accidental and coincidental influences. This conditioning starts while still sucking at the mother's breast. Our conditioning is the result of an ACCIDENT OF BIRTH over which we have absolutely no control.

We grow up to become a part of the vast majority, with identical values in regard to most of our thinking, beliefs, dress, etc. as those around us, according to our accident of birth. Our inculturation deals with such concepts as justice, equality, fairness, freedom, honesty, self-sacrificing selfishness and all moral values. Without such preconditioning, no one would join any extremist group. I refer to the 100% patriots who fight communism; the revolutionaries who become martyrs for the proletariat; members of the Ku Klux Klan, who represent themselves as the guardians of white Christian supremacy; the terrorists, the assassinator of Indira Ghandi, Premier of India in 1984, the Kennedy brothers and Rev. Martin Luther King; or any of the Libyan or Palestinian suicide squads of hijackers. The actions of all the foregoing were the result of the sum total of their lifelong conditioning, which include genetics, accident of birth and chance influences that occur later in life.

Thus, we are conditioned to sacrifice ourselves for the good of the common whole, society, and culture. Your own deep self-drives, your individual well-being and the price you must pay (losing your life, limbs, eyesight, in war; your stomach ache, ulcers, sexual impotency, etc.) is indeed considered unfortunate by society. You are indoctrinated with the belief that you must sacrifice yourself on the altar of the common good. In short, your conditioning says, "die...get ulcers...develop colitis...loose a limb or even get your head shot off...The Purple Heart awaits your surviving family." Living by established standards and values—to be patriotic and will willing to die for you country, believe in God, the family, future generations, etc.—society accepts, respects, reveres you. Society's values must be number one on the totem pole. It must never be you. To do so is frowned upon as SELFISH. It is my firm belief that society respects you when you are SELFLESS.

I do not sit in judgment of the conditioning process described in the foregoing. I simply state the undeniable fact that this is how you become humanized. This very process of humanization creates problems and conflicts that have deep ramification throughout your entire life. Even though you are not conscious of those repressed forbidden parts of yourself, they are forever part of your psyche with the tendency to impact on your perception and behavior. They not only appear in your dreams, but also in your irrational behavior and/or neurotic symptoms. There is an unavoidable collision and conflict between your two selves, i.e., the one self that is concealed, (seeking an outlet both in your overt life as well as in your fantasy dream life), and the other self that adapted to your environment. This conflict lasts throughout your life. Each of us has a different degree of tolerance for how much of forbidden aggression is allowed to emerge into consciousness. This depends on the degree to which you can cope with the guilt associated with the release of forbidden aggression.

I now ask you to stop reading for a few minutes to ponder the concept that follows. Try to recapture the feeling of terror and the fear of annihilation you had when you were one, two or three years old, a period in your life when your survival was determined by the disciplinarian parents. Let your imagination take over. The feeling must sink in so deeply that it gets to your gut. This is what you must do in order to fully feel the

HUMANIZATION process. It is important to feel this terror because to the irrational unconscious, that perceives a molehill as a mountain, what is repressed is a threat to your survival. It is precisely this intense, unconscious fear that is at the root of the phenomenon of RESISTANCE, as it exists in psychoanalysis. This applies not only to your patients, but also to you, the psychotherapist, when doing your own self-analysis.

STOP READING

At the outset of this chapter I discussed how guilt and punishment are a threat to our survival. By the time we reach post adolescent adulthood, there is already an established HOMEOSTASIS between one's aggression, the guilt related to the aggression and the punishment. I named this homeostasis phenomenon, THE AGP SYNDROME (AGGRESSION-GUILT-PUNISHMENT) This phenomenon is so important in The Moss Method for Self-Analysis, that I devote the entire Chapter 7 to deal with it.

In the next chapter I shall present three case histories to illustrate phenomena described in this chapter. The latter will demonstrate the dynamics of how the unconscious deals with threatening situations.

CHAPTER 4

KEEP THE SHOW ON THE ROAD

The three case histories presented in this chapter illustrate the dynamics involved when conditions in one's life become a reality with which it is impossible to cope. I characterized this dilemma as Impossible to Cope with Reality phenomenon (ICR).[9] The three cases that follow illustrate the impact of the unconscious on one's life when an ICR exists. Familiarity with the ICR phenomenon is an absolute prerequisite for the Moss Method of self-analysis.

1) The Case of Little Joey: Joey, a three and a half year old boy, seemed to be normal in every respect except for the fact that he had occasional temper tantrums. His parents were unhappily married during the six years before Joey was born. They were considering separation. Thus, Joey came as an unwanted child. His mother, a neurotic woman, now perceived herself trapped in a bad marriage. In this environment and with this type of mother, it is obvious that Joey hardly could have received the

---

9   The abbreviation ICR, is used throughout this text to represent the Impossible-to-cope-wth phenomenon.

kind of spiritual love and warmth so important during his form-ative years. When Little Joey was three and one half years old he experienced a crisis that had a profound effect on his life. A baby sister was born. Joey's parents believed they had prepared him properly to accept the new family member by explaining to him about the coming event. To Joey's childish mind, this prepara-tion by the parents was only an abstraction. The latter became a reality when the sibling arrived home from the hospital and descended upon the household. He perceived his sister as a rival; one who robbed him of his mother's love, of which he never received enough to satisfy him even before the new arrival. That limited love must now be divided with his rival, his sibling. What made it worse was that he perceived his rival receiving the giant share.—This, of course, is the reasonable pre-sumption of how Joey perceived it all.—Joey expressed his anger, hostility and indignation in a number of different ways. For the first few weeks, his hatred was only verbal, but later he threatened to "kill her by stabbing her with a knife." At one time he actually grabbed his infant sister by her throat in an attempt to choke her. In the beginning the parents were relatively patient with Joey, explaining that "the baby was an addition to the fam-ily and needed love and affection as much as you do." But when Joey's actions turned towards physical violence, the parents took a firmer disciplinary attitude. They spanked him frequently, sending him to his room to stay there until he became a good boy.

This entire situation was a dilemma that Joey could not cope with; i.e., he was barely getting enough love to satisfy his insecure needs before his enemy rival became a part of the household. Now he was getting even less love than before. His hatred for his mother and sister was the only way he could react to this intolerable situation. But when he manifested his hostility, he received even less love than before. The situation developed into a crisis of major proportion for Joey. He was being punished for emotions that he could not control. There was no way out of this dilemma. He was plagued with frustration, hostility, guilt and fear of punishment. Joey was in a situation with which he could not cope. As Joey's predicament worsened, his behavior became more intolerable to his parents. The punishment threatened his survival. (as explained in the previous chapter)

Confronted with an ICR, after a period of about five weeks, Joey underwent a profound change in his entire behavior. It was a personality conversion. He no longer hated his baby sister. He now showed her affection. At times, he even caressed her. He told 'mummy' how happy he was to have the new baby in the family. He seemed to be totally reconciled to taking second place in his mother's affections. But accompanying this change, there were other changes that occurred: Joey started bed wetting; he reverted to the baby talk similar to when he was six months old; he became withdrawn; at times he had a far-away look with an expression of resigned detachment; he became a thumb sucker, his right thumb was constantly in his mouth. What follows is an explanation of the change resulting from Joey's confrontation with an ICR.

The sibling rivalry dilemma was a reality with which Joey was incapable of coping. When he showed his hatred he was not only denied what little love he was getting, he was also punished. Nature stepped in and came to the rescue with the phenomenon of REGRESSION. This is what always happens when confronted with an ICR. Thus, in Joey's psyche, it was as if time were turned back to when he was an infant; a reality when he was his mother's only child and had no rival sibling. In this fantasy world he received all the love of his mother that he was denied in the real world. In his regressed state he had no need to hate his sister which had gotten him into so much trouble with his parents. Reality was REPRESSED by the involuntary regression phenomenon, thus, assuring his survival. He was no longer threatened with annihilation.[10]

The conscious hostility, which in this case was the natural and normal response to an intolerable situation, was forbidden and dangerous to Joey. The conflict brought on a crisis which resulted in the ICR phenomenon. There was no longer any hostility in his overt behavior because now his hostility became a CONVERSION SYMPTOM. This phenomenon of repression and regression, and conversion symptoms, is a prototype of a phenomenon that is a common occurrence throughout our lives when we deal with a reality that we can't cope with, i.e., an ICR phenomenon.

A person is able to deny a reality by the use of magical powers of the unconscious mind. We often see this when catastrophe strikes an individual who can't cope with it. Examples of ICR phenomena are the following: death of a loved one, the loss of financial fortune; a serious accident with the loss of part of one's body; to some individuals even the loss of a job or livelihood due to illness or unemployment; loss of one's home and bankruptcy, etc. The list of situations go on to fill many pages. Because the psyche exists in the fantasy world of the past, an individual confronted with an ICR relates to that reality as though he/she were hypnotized and regressed to become the past self, a time when the current reality did not exist; but with a posthypnotic suggestion to remain the same current self. Thus, anytime one represses the pain of the traumatic reality, i.e., when confronted with an ICR phenomenon, one tends to react similar to what occurred with Little Joey. The symptoms that arise replace the repressed emotions. That is why such symptoms are

---

10 See chapter 3, *Huminization of the Beast.*

called CONVERSION SYMPTOMS. When conversion symptoms arise, one rarely connects the repressed emotion with the resulting symptom.[11] In order to rid oneself of psychosomatic or neurotic symptoms—stomach tension, migraine headaches, all sorts of phobias, colitis, stuttering, compulsive eating or smoking, sexual impotency or frigidity, etc.—the analyst must presume the existence of an ICR. Successful therapy exposes and deals with the repressed emotions/conflicts resulting from an ICR. Psychoanalysis is a modality that shows the connection between the ICR and the patient's symptoms.

(2) The Case of Sailor Jones as reported by Lewis Wolberg:[12] Jones was a man 26 years of age. He was in the US Navy during World War 11, assigned to a ship that was torpedoed. He was one of 40 survivors among the 500 seamen on that ship. He managed to escape to a life raft. The ship split in two and sank about 150 yards away. It was a horribly gruesome experience to witness many of his buddies lost as the ship disappeared from sight. Several days after this disaster, sailor Jones was afflicted with a violent tic. He developed a jerk of his right shoulder together with a violent twitch of the right arm. He underwent psychiatric treatment when he arrived at the base hospital about one month later. His therapy was HYPNOANALYSIS, a modality developed by Dr. Lewis Wolberg, consisting of hypnosis combined with psychoanalysis. After many months of treatment, material was revealed for which he had had total amnesia.

During his treatment he recalled the explosion from the torpedo attack of his ship. He then recalled that emergency alarms, sirens and horns blasted loudly ordering all men back to their stations.

---

11 Engel, Geroge L.; *The Psychoanalytical Approach to Psychosomatic Medicine*; Basic Books Inc., New York, p. 252.

12 Lewis Wolberg, MD, *Hypnoanalysis*; Grune and Straton Pub. Co., 1945.

He started back towards his station in accordance with his training.—Sailor Jones' duty and responsibilities for responding to emergencies became a conditioned reflex. Practice exercises were done almost daily during the period of his training, reinforced by constant maintenance drills. When the sirens blasted during the mock emergencies, Sailor Jones would automatically hasten to his station below deck and automatically turn off certain engine valves.—

Sailor Jones was in the act of carrying out his duties and responsibilities. On his way to the engine room he stopped dead in his tracks. Terror struck like a thunderbolt. He had a panic seizure. Death stared him in the face. He broke out into a cold sweat and for one instant froze in his tracks. The only thought he had was to save his life. He made an about-face and headed for the upper deck where the life rafts were located. He never gave a thought to the criminal nature of his actions. Through the confusion that prevailed he succeeded in getting on one of the life rafts. When the threat of imminent death ceased to exist, a markedly adverse reaction occurred, i.e., he started trembling and retching. He heaved up his guts. He was wracked with guilt. He wished that he had stayed on board and had remained at his station where he should have been. He blamed himself for the fate of his buddies. It never occur to him that there was nothing he might have done that would have saved the ship and the 460 lives of his fellow crew.

He was obsessed with the thought, "If only I had gone back to my station and performed my duty of turning off the valves." He was overwhelmed with guilt because he failed in the responsibility for which he was trained, rehearsed and conditioned. "The lives of so many depended on me and I was derelict," he lamented to his therapist during subsequent treatment. He was irrationally convinced that it was his dereliction of duty that was responsible for the sinking of the ship. He kept repeating how he wished he had gone back and turned those valves off, even if it meant losing his life. He was torn with agony and remorse. He couldn't live with that heavy guilt load: "...four humdred sixty men lost their lives on account of me," was his lament. He became suicidal for a period of several weeks. His suicidal obsession disappeared when he developed the tic.

Nature intervened performing her magic—as she did with Little Joey—to make it possible for Sailor Jones to cope with the reality. In his unconscious psyche, time was turned back as though he were hypnotically regressed. His fantasies were that he was at his station turning off the valves with using his right hand. This is the area of his body where he developed the tic. With this magical fantasy in his regressed state, he lost all recollection of the incident. The guilt disappeared. He developed complete and total amnesia for the entire grueling experience. The amnesia lasted until the time he was in therapy. But with amnesia and freedom from guilt, he developed a tic. His twitching right arm from hand to shoulder symbolically represented turning off the valves in the engine room. Thus, Sailor Jones was able to function again. The conversion symptom was his defense against a devastating guilt that made him suicidal. Regression to a guiltless past was nature's "magic" that saved Sailor Jones from total collapse. He was no longer suicidal. The tic, a conversion symptom, was finally eliminated by therapeutically reversing the process of regression, i.e., his recollection and reexperiencing the entire horrible catastrophy, including all the crushing guilt. By therapeutically strengthening his ego, he was able to deal with the guilt. The tic ceased because he no longer needed the neurotic defense, i.e., the symptoms.

3) The Case of Aunt Margie. Aunt Margie was a woman, 40 years of age, when she suddenly started to stutter. She was distressed and bewildered because she had never done so before. With analytic investigation she revealed she started stuttering two weeks after she got into a shouting altercation with her mother. "I wish I knew how to get rid of you," [her words] she yelled to her mother as she left her mother's house, slamming the door behind her. She told me that she had feelings of getting rid of her mother every time they argued. As with past altercations she forgot about the incident. In the meantime she was told that her mother had undergone a medical check up because of blood in her stool. The diagnosis was hopeless malignancy of the colon that had already metastasized to other organs. Her life expectancy was about six months.

Two weeks after she learned of the diagnosis, Aunt Margie recalled the argument with her mother. She was obsessed with the belief that she was responsible for her mother's cancer. After about a week of this obsessive guilt, she forgot the argument, i.e., she developed amnesia. And with the latter, the guilt and everything associated with the incident of the confrontation, became repressed from her consciousness. During the analytic session she described her mother as "a troublesome neurotic. She made my life miserable." [Margie's words]. Her mothers death would have liberated her. Without a doubt, Aunt Margie had an unconscious death wish for her mother. But such a wish was never felt consciously. But in its place she was afflicted with stuttering. In effect, she regressed to a time before she had those evil thoughts. She struck herself dumb, symbolized by the stuttering.[13] Here again, the CONVERSION SYMPTOM was the result of the repression of a deep, oppressive, intolerable guilt that resulted in an ICR phenomenon.

The three case histories cited have one thing in common, namely, that in each case the unresolved conflict or the emotional pain was so intense, that function would have ceased and an emotional breakdown would have occurred if nature had not intervened. By means of regression, the impossible reality was replaced by a past period of life when such reality did not exist. In so doing two things result: 1) the individual continues to function, e.g., THE SHOW STAYS ON THE ROAD. 2) Conversion symptoms develop. In the previous chapter, I have discussed how by the age of five, we already have a highly developed repressive mechanism. Feeling forbidden emotions becomes a threat to one's survival. These threatening emotions are repressed. In their place, and on a conscious level, very opposite emotions replace that which is forbidden. Thus, very early in life, one is already a FUGITIVE FROM ONE'S OWN SELF!

The next chapter deals with sexuality. I shall discuss why this is a powerhouse force in yourself just as it is in your patients; how it impacts on areas of your life without any cognizance of the connection.

---

13 An unconscious, parental death wish is a very common fantasy of adults who have dependent, bothersome, ailing parents. (Death wishes can also exist for ailing and troublesome spouses; and sometimes for one's seriously mentally, or disabled child.) Though death would liberate the caretaker, such wishes must be repressed in our culture because it is considered despicable and unthinkable. But when there is such an unconscious wish, when the parent/spouse/child dies, there is generally a very marked emotional reaction, as though the wish were the cause of death.

CHAPTER 5

NATURE'S OBSESSION WITH SEX

The premise upon which this chapter is based is that the most powerful instinct (force or drive) of all life is the SURVIVAL of the SPECIES. This instinct has two aspects that are different yet intimately related and overlapping. 1) The survival of the individual organism;[14] 2) The survival of the species. The survival of the individual organism serves the purpose to give new life to a successor, thereby to perpetuate the species. When a species becomes extinct, one can assume that nature has failed in her experiment with that particular species. Over the billions of years that our planet exists, only those species that were able to adapt to the relentlessly cruel changing environment were able to survive. Up to now, the human species has been one of the fortunate.

The survival instinct is as real a force of nature as any, the gravitational forces that keep the celestial bodies in their orbits, and the force within the atom and the powerful force of the

---

14 Chester, Eustice; *Salvation Through Sex*; quote from *The Life and Work of Wilhem Reich*; William Morrow & Co; New York, 1973 p. 82.

Niagara Falls. Each species has evolved a means of reproduction. Nature resorts to a great variety of modalities and methods. For example, some plants use pollination; some animals produce eggs that are fertilized by sperm either inside the body or outside. For mammals it is copulation (coitus, sexual intercourse). The following is how Wardon, Jenkins and Warner regard the force of species survival:

> One of the fundamental characteristics of living systems is the tendency to give rise to new types from time to time under appropriate conditions. The revolution of new species usually requires a relatively long period of time. Once life begins, the continuity of life evolves as the most powerful force...certain biological forms of fitness find the ultimate means for the survival of the species....[15]

> In view of the tremendously powerful force of species perpetuation, it would be unrealistic to take issue with the fact that in the human animal, the force of reproduction, i.e., the sex drive, is the most powerful of all the forces that motivates our thoughts and behavior. R.S. De Rope says, "The biologic necessity to ensure the perpetuation of the human species was assured by sexuality."[16]

It is not only the Freudian analysts who claim that humankind's sexuality is all pervasive, but also down through the ages, poets, artists and troubadours have sung and written about this force. I believe that De Rope says it exactly right, "Sex energy soaring beautifully, etherealized, a spiritual flame uniting two in one, transcending the flesh, a symbol of mystical blending sex energy,

---

15 Wardon, C.J. Jenkins &, T.N Warner, H.W. *Comparative Psychology*; Ronald Press, New York; 1925 p. 102.
16 De Rope, R.S.; *The Sexual Force in Man and Animals*; Delacorte Press; New York; 1969, p.102.

a universal biological urge with no other function than to bring about the union of gametes, the active moving sperm of the male, the large inactive egg cell of the female...All this and a good deal more is implied in the term, sex energy...It spreads out like an ameba in all directions, transcends the purely biologic, enters the realms of art, pathology, religion, morality, ethics and metaphysics. It shows itself in everything... If the mind of contemporary man is obsessed by this force let us admit that there is a reason for the obsession, *for nature itself is obsessed*[17] [emphasis mine].

Freud discovered that all psychoanalytic patients, if allowed to talk freely and without any direction or interference from the therapist, will eventually discuss their sexual conflicts, frustrations, guilt, disappointment, perversion, etc., providing that the therapists is non-directional and is free of moral judgment or criticism.[18] This has been reaffirmed by every practicing psycho-analyst. I have found this to be true with my patients whom I have treated analytically. Those therapists who direct the patient's attention away from their otherwise free association, naturally, will not always encounter this eventual emergence of sexuality with the same regularity and consistency as the Freudian analyst. When one does self-analysis, one should always search and suspect a sexual component regardless of whether or not it is present at the start of the session. What now follows is why and how this all pervasive force intrudes and manifests itself in the manner described.

The foregoing discussion is a brief attempt to set the back-ground for one born and raised in the Judeo-Christian culture.

---

17 Ibid

18 Freud, Sig. *Three Essays on Theory of Sexuality:*, (1905) Standard Edition , 7123-245, 1959

How the latter affects us can best be described in the words of William G. Cole:

> Christianity, smelted in the same cultural crucible as Judaism, inherited Judaic sex phobias and Judaic fears of the sexual organs and the sexual act. It also accepted the Judaic belief that Jehovah had created the earth and 'desired it to be filled with living beings. It is a short step to condemning the enjoyment of sexual intercourse without conception i.e., the banning of the pill. The Christian church had to accept that sexual intercourse was necessary for God's purpose, but could not free itself from the belief that sexual intercourse was basically sinful. Anything so enjoyable must be. One could be granted indulgence for it only if one produced a child. Christian theologians even suspected the virtue of women who had been raped. The victims could be forgiven only if they could swear or prove that they had not enjoyed the experience.[19]

Leon Salzman states: "...penile erection is often visible at birth."[20] Today there is evidence that even in the womb, the fetus already is experiencing sexual activity. This has been demonstrated by the use of sonograms that show erection in the male fetus.[21] Is there a mother who has not seen the boy infant with an erection, smiling, laughing and enjoying his dreams even in early infancy? All children above one year of age are already masturbating with visible expressions of pleasure. Unmistakable

---

19 Cole, William, G.; *Sex in Christianity and Psychoanalysis*; Oxford University Press, 1983. p59

20 Salzmlan, Leon; *Sexuality in Psychoanalytic*; Basic Books, 1968, p.128

21 Money, J. and Tucker, P.: *Sexual Signatures*, Little, Brown and Co., Boston (1975), p. 135.

sexual fantasies of very young children are easily observed in their games and in their play with themselves and with each other.

Until repetitive conditioning occurs, a child must be mystified relative to the reasons for punishment. It would not stretch the imagination too much to presume the young child, who does not yet know why it is being chastised, instinctively and unconsciously relates the punishment to ongoing sexual fantasies. Thus, the seeds of sexual guilt are already planted early in life. The sexual guilt is reinforced later by overt threats and admonitions directed at the child seen masturbating. Some enlightened parents think they are smart or wise by saying nothing to the child, but simply taking the child's hands away from its genitals, or by trying to distract the child into doing something else. But after dozens of this kind of charade, with the passage of time, the cumulative effect is to condition the child to associate its genitals with something forbidden, evil or dirty. The sum total of the foregoing is to ultimately affect the child so that consciously or otherwise it eventually reacts to sexuality as evil, dirty and forbidden

How much worse is it for those less informed parents who overtly reprimand, threaten or even punish the child for masturbation. Need I remind you of the deliberately evasive attitude of many parents when it comes to sex talk in the home? They change the subject when children ask about sex. What comes to the mind of the child when sexual discussion between adults is abruptly terminated when the child unexpectedly enters the room? The ongoing Clinton sexual scandal does not escape the attention of the vast TV audience of children.[22] Imagine what must go on in the minds of so many children when parents turn off the TV so that their children do not see the lurid and salacious details. There are reports of many children asking their

---

22 Occuring during the latter part of 1998.

parents to tell them what oral sex is. The parent's confusion and embarrassment does not escape the child. The child soon learns that talk or questions about sex is wrong. But this doesn't stop the child's sexual thoughts and fantasies, which now are invested with guilt, confusion and conflict. Notwithstanding the latter, the force and power of the child's sexuality is so great that absolutely nothing can alter the child's sexual fantasies, even under the most oppressive discipline.

Nothing escapes the young child and its curiosity to know about sex, the most powerful life force of the human being. Most conditioning of a child is subliminal in nature and therefore entirely below the level of consciousness or awareness-not only for the child but also for the parents. Their attitudes and behavior are part of the subliminal conditioning process. Parents are oblivious of how their own attitudes influence and are passed on to their child.

But whether one is aware or not, it does not alter the conditioned reflex effect that such exposure has on the child's attitude towards sex.[23] This conditioning that occurs long before the child is five years old is further reinforced by educational institutions, religious institutions, and the entire judicial/legal system with its attitudes towards sex. There are dozens of rules and regulations in my own Hebrew religion relative to the female 'cleansing' herself by her visits to the mikvah—the baptismal bath—to which each woman must subject herself after menstruation and before sleeping with her husband. I have been told by an Irish Catholic woman that the sisters at her parochial school "drilled into me that sex was evil and dirty, not to be enjoyed. It is the wifely duty to submit to the animalistic, bestial needs of the

---

23 Sandler,J.; *On the Concept of the Superego; Psycholgy Study of the Child;* p163, 1962

husband." Need I remind the reader how the authorities bear down on progressive and enlightened school teachers who attempt to teach and educate their students about sex.[24] The media is replete with cases where teachers have not only been reprimanded and harassed, but have even been dismissed for attempting sexual education.

Apropos to the above, I digress to describe an experience I had at the age of eight. The reader might see this as ludicrously funny if it weren't for the fact that it was traumatic for me. I was in the third grade when the following occurred: my teacher, Miss Smith, a spinster about forty-five years of age, summoned me, very sternly, from my seat and asked me to follow her. She left the classroom. I tagged behind her, mystified as she walked grimly to the end of the corridor. There was a door that opened into a janitor's closet with his pails and mops. and a large low sink with a water faucet. The stony faced teacher did not utter a single word until we were both in the closet. She then turned on the water. She then produced a wooden 12 inch ruler that I had not noticed until that moment. She put one end of the ruler into my right hand ordering me to hold it firmly. She then shoved my left hand under the running water. I was totally baffled about what was happening. She broke her silence and spoke for the first time. "Smack your hand with the ruler," she ordered me in an angry, stern voice. 1 was paralyzed with fear and did nothing. She then grabbed my hand that was holding the ruler and started to strike my other hand, which she kept pushing under the running water. "Harder, harder," she demanded. This went on for about two or three minutes. To this very day I can hear those harsh, cruel words, "harder, harder." At no time, from the very beginning to the very end, did she tell me what this was all about and why I was put through this bewildering ordeal.

---

24 ibid; p144.

I forgot the entire experience until over a quarter of a century later when I was on an analytic couch. It was presumed that Miss Smith must have caught me masturbating. What else could it have been? This presumption is based on the fact that I remember as far back as my first year in school, I would get a pleasant sensation by rubbing my small but firm penis against the side of the desk. It is likely that I "played" with my penis, i.e., masturbated, but this I can't remember. These recollections emerged on the analytic couch. The fact that I recalled this incident after repressing it for so long indicates the degree of trauma the foregoing must have been to me. I now return to the body of the text.

Though the sexual fantasies of a five year old child are already invested with some degree of evil, taboo, anxiety and guilt, this does not stop the child from experiencing, and living out these fantasies in her/his play, dreams, etc. Absolutely nothing can stop such fantasies from occurring. These biological functions take place under any and all environmental conditions or discipline, regardless of the intensity of the latter. It is important to realize that because sexual fantasies cannot be prevented by any oppressive environment, they become invested with guilt. Early childhood sexual guilt remains lodged in the unconscious for the rest of our lives. By the time we are adults, we have learned that sex is permissible under certain conditions, such as marriage. However, the guilt in our unconscious is permanent as though chiseled in stone. In Chapter 2, "The Magical Power of the Unconscious," I described in detail how whatever happens in one's life remains forever in one's unconscious. Thus, whether or not you are cognizant of your sexual guilt, it can never be removed from your unconscious mind, even though you do not remember any such thoughts, activity or guilt of your childhood past. Analytic probing will uncover and bring to awareness sexual thoughts and emotions of childhood sexuality.

Repressed sexual guilt often interferes with healthy, normal sexual function. In the male adult it is manifested by anxiety of performance much more than in the female. The reason is obvious since sexual failure in the male is more obvious. He must have an erection in order to penetrate the vagina. Also, ejaculation of semen accompanies his orgasm. The female, by contrast, needs no physically demonstrable prerequisite to engage in sexual intercourse, i.e., to receive the erect penis. She does not stand exposed to failure as does the sexually impotent male. Apropos of this, there is an anecdote about the woman who told her friend, another woman, that if she had to have an erection every time she engaged in sex with her husband, he would have thrown her out a long time ago.

It is a known fact that some creative artists experience guilt and anxiety during the process of their creative activity. By means of the psychoanalysis, the artist becomes aware of the relationship between his/her guilt and anxiety and sexual fantasies. I have experienced this with several of my own artist patients. The very act of creation draws its force and energy from one's sexual drive. The literature is replete with examples. Composing a sonata like Beethoven's Kreutzer Sonata, doing a great painting or sculpture, advanced higher mathematics, writing a book or composing a poem, are all creative processes that draw their energy from the act of creation of new life, i.e., sexuality. The foregoing does not apply to one who is a craftsman or garden variety of imitative artist. Susan Sontag makes quite a distinction between the latter type of artist and the genuinely creative artist.[25]

---

25 Sontag, Susan; Against Interpretation. Farrar, Strauss & Giroux; 1981

Since all guilt is equated to a threat to one's survival, especially sexual guilt, the threat is canceled with sexual failure. Failure is brought about by regression, an unconscious and involuntary phenomenon to a pre-Oedipal period in life when one's genital sexuality has not yet developed. The foregoing explains why consciously one strives for sexual success, often accompanied by over-anxiety, while on an unconscious level, failure, the negation of sex, assures survival. Intensified anxiety, often referred to as PERFORMANCE ANXIETY, always indicates unconscious guilt with an *unconscious* wish for sexual failure. It is my opinion that insight (through the analytic process) of the unconscious relationship between sexual guilt and the wish for failure is a far more effective aphrodisiac than the currently popular viagra.

The biological force of youth generally is able to overcome the obstacle of sexual guilt. But as you grow older, past the age of forties and fifties, when your sex drive lessens, the unconscious obstacle becomes more dominant than the sex drive. Sexual failure begins to replace satisfying sex. With repeated failures, you ultimately lose your sexual interest. I am firmly convinced that were it not for the obstacle of sexual guilt, we all would be sexually active throughout our entire lives. My own active sex at age 89 is due to the fact that during my self-analysis I deal with sexual guilt, which to this day continues to be present in my unconscious. By analytic insight, I cancel out the adverse, negative impact that my guilt would have on my sexuality. I remove the obstacle to achieve normal, healthy sex. Having reached old age, I try to have a self-analysis session prior to anticipated sexual activity. Successful self-analysis is an effective aphrodisiac that always works for me, as it would for you. What is remarkable about the foregoing is that in my forties and fifties my sexual experiences were mostly a frustrating failure. My motive in discussing my sexuality is to demonstrate to you, my colleagues, the potential of self-analysis as a life style. Sexual fulfillment is another benefit you will derive from self-analysis in addition to becoming a better analyst.

In the foregoing I dealt with the following:

1) Survival of the species is the most powerful drive of all life. In the human species, this translates into our sexual drive.
2) In our culture, starting early in life, one is inculcated with sexual guilt, which remains in one's unconscious forever.
3) Unconscious sexual guilt is an obstacle to normal, healthy sexual function.
4) Creativity in art, science, industry etc., derives its energy from the sublimation of one's powerful sexual drive. Likewise neurotic symptoms often have their roots in disturbed sexual function.
5) You may have a serious sexual obstacle in your unconscious, yet you may be totally oblivious of it. Very often, only through psychoanalysis can you become cognizant of this obstacle.
6) Removal of the obstacle by means of analytic insight tends to result in successful sex.

I close this chapter with the emphasis that the force of one's sexuality is a power house of stored energy. Like the power of dammed up water, it always finds a course for going downstream. Likewise, dynamic sexual power can not be dammed up. It can be sublimated into channels of useful productivity and/or creativity; or, sexual force could be expended in neurotic symptoms including sexual failure and other character disorders. Generally speaking, it is only through psychoanalysis that we can become aware of the connection between our emotional disturbances (and/or our neurotic symptoms) and our dammed up sexual force. Therefore, in doing self-analysis, you must always suspect that your illusive sexuality is lurking somewhere concealed in your mind, unbeknown to you. You must look for it.

CHAPTER 6

WE ARE ALL HYPNOTIC SUBJECTS

This chapter consists of a discussion of hypnotic phenomenon to illustrate two phenomena: how our unconscious impacts on our perception and behavior; how we are conditioned to behave as though we were hypnotized early in life. Although we believe that our perceptions and behavior are under our control, I shall attempt to show that this is not always the case. There are times that unknowingly we act as if we are responding to a posthypnotic suggestion. When this happens, we find rational reasons for what we are do, totally oblivious of the unconscious motivation. The unconscious also has the power to censor or select from reality, what we see, smell or hear. A subject under hypnosis with his eyes closed will be told that upon opening his eyes he will see a picture of his mother but will have no recollection of the posthypnotic suggestion. Then, when he opens his eyes and is shown a blank sheet of paper, he will describe his mother's face in minute detail. This is a positive hallucination. The next time under hypnosis he is shown a photo, but told that when he opens his eyes he will see a blank piece of paper. This is a negative hallucination. People sometimes hear their fortune teller say things that never was said, or do not hear what were said. What follows is an illustration of how you may rationalize your behavior yet be completely oblivious of the motivation originating in your unconscious. The illustration will also demonstate selective censorship, a phenomenon that is discussed when dealing with the Moss Method of Self-analysis.

A cartoon in The New Yorker Magazine depicts a scene in a gallery of a museum in which a spinsterly woman paints on a canvas mounted on an easel.[26] She is reproducing a small portion of an immense mural that filled an entire wall. The mural depicts a caveman wearing only a loincloth, carrying under his left arm a naked young woman, her wild hair flying in the wind and her body pressed closely to his side. She had a gleeful expression on her face. In his right hand he holds the legendary club. The abductor is about to enter the mouth of a cave, located on the side of a hill, proudly carrying the spoils of his victory. The landscape is clustered with shrubs and trees. The foliage is so thick that the entrance to the cave is barely discernable. To one side of the mural, near the upper left hand corner, is a small bird perched on a tree twig. It is only this bird that the spinster is reproducing on her canvas. She seems to be completely oblivious of everything else in the mural. Could anyone doubt that her interest in the bird is motivated by the abduction? More specifically, wouldn't you agree that there is an unconscious identification with the abducted woman? If you would ask her why she chose to reproduce this particular bird, she most certainly would give an explanation totally oblivious of any unconscious motivation, such as the color, size or shape of its feathers, beak or some other insignificant detail. Her answer may not convince you, even

26 The New Yorker Magazine; April 14, 1983, p.43.

though she would be certain of her reason. It is apparent that the naive woman was totally oblivious of the fact that a bird is often a phallic symbol.

To further illustrate how you may be totally oblivious of your unconscious motivation, I shall fall back on my twenty-five years of experience as a practicing hypnotist, during which time I have experimented with all aspects of hypnotic phenomena. It is very common to give a person who is in the hypnotic state a posthypnotic suggestion to perform a certain act upon recovering from the hypnotic state. The posthypnotic suggestion is often accompanied by another suggestion of total amnesia for whatever happened while under hypnosis.

What follows is such an experiment that I have performed dozens of times for professional audiences: A subject under hypnosis, is given a posthypnotic suggestion that in ten minutes she/he will open the window across the room. He/she will not remember that it is a posthypnotic suggestion. Upon awakening the subject looks at her/his watch periodically so that in approximately ten minutes the subject goes to the window and proceeds to open it. If asked why she/he is opening the window, the subject answers that she/he feels warm and uncomfortable, or that the room is stuffy, or some other rational and legitimate reason. I have seen many instances in which the subject actually sweated with visible beads of perspiration on the forehead. The subject may even open her/his collar. These reactions are not faked. They are the result of suggestions lodged in the unconscious and are genuine physiological responses (sweating. discomfort or even pain). The changes result from 'physiological enslavement' by the compulsive need to carry out the posthypnotic suggestion. This indicates how your physiology and/or behavior is dominated by your unconscious. Although the onlooker witnessing the experiment observes how the subject is totally dominated by unconscious compulsive behavior, the subject is totally oblivious of the later due to the posthypnotic suggestion of amnesia.

This experiment can be done with any number of variations of posthypnotic suggestions. What follows is a list of potential posthypnotic suggestions that may be performed and how the subject might respond when asked the reason for his/her actions:

1 Remove your shoes: Reason: "My tight shoes hurt my feet."
2 Drink two glasses of water: Reason: "I ate someathing salty just before I came here. I always have two glasses of water after I eat salty food."
3 Lie down and rest: Reason: "I wasn't feeling well when I woke up this morning. I always rest when this happens."
4. Make a phone call to one's spouse (or mother or sister): Reason: "I wanted to know whether the new T.V. was delivered."
5 Walk out of the room: Reason: "The room is stuffy. Don't you feel it?"

Although the answers given may be spontaneous fabrications, it must not be construed as willful or intentional lying. This type of behavior is often seen in everyday life with others; perhaps even with you and me. Compulsive thinking and/or behavior is almost always justified by real or fabricated reasons. The unconscious has the capacity to play tricks on us, i.e., manipulate our intellect with rational reasoning when compulsive behavior exists, i.e., unconsciously motivated behavior. In the hypnotic experiments, compulsive behavior is planted in the unconscious by the posthypnotic suggestions. The latter can result in the following: 1) changes in motor capacity (increase or decrease in muscular strength, paralysis of muscles, increase or decrease in salivary flow, flushing or blanching of the skin, etc.) 2) changes in sensation; (feeling excessive heat, cold, pain, anesthesia, diminished or increased visual acuity, alteration in sense of smell, taste; or even the need to urinate, or to vomit) 3) alteration of emotional state (depression, elation, anger, guilt, fear, anxiety, inferiority, superiority, cowardice, courage or cockiness, mistrust and suspicion, erotic stimulation or sexual impotence, a feeling of being rejected, abused, cheated, etc.) The different kinds of alterations that can be induced are almost unlimited.

I once had a very timid woman warble like a bird when in the hypnotic state; then I told her that she was an opera singer. She sang and performed outlandish vocal sounds. Once I performed a demonstration for a parent-teacher group. The subject was a mathematics teacher. I gave him a posthypnotic suggestion "to feel and act as smart as Albert Einstein." With the usual posthypnotic suggestion of amnesia I awakened him. He beamed with a smug smile telling me how smart he was. He even asked me to test him. He would rattle off wrong answers to my questions. Yet he acted arrogantly, as though he were right. For example one question was to multiply 5,469 by 4,594. Or what is the square root of 1,352? After allowing him to show his pride and conceit and several more questions, I again put him in a trance. But this time the posthypnotic suggestion was to be and act stupid. After awakening him from the second trance, his facial expression became moronic. He could not spell his name, nor could he count from one to ten without making a mistake. He was not faking. He was simply motivated by an unconscious force resulting from posthypnotic suggestions.

The foregoing discussion on hypnosis is intended to give you a different perspective of irrational perception, irrational thinking, and/or neurotic symptoms. At birth you have no image of yourself. How you perceive yourself is the result of accumulated and collected stimuli that bounce off your environment, primarily your parents (or parent substitutes. An individual's self-image, negative or positive, is as though he/she was hypnotized by his/her parents who were 'long range' hypnotists.[27] Thus, FOR THE REST OF YOUR LIFE, your self esteem will simulate that of a hypnotized individual. *For the rest of your life* also applies to any feeling/belief or prejudice that you ever had; i.e., the latter will also remain in your unconscious forever. I have had atheist patients who were shocked when on the analytic couch to discovered that in their unconscious, they were not only believers but they were also superstitious and believed in magic. It is even more shocking for you, the analyst, who is liberated from such prejudices to discover racism continues to lurk in your unconscious. What is in the unconscious remains there forever and may affect your behavior, perception and belief simulating posthypnotic suggestions.

The degree to which our intellect is influenced by our unconscious is illustrated by the public's reaction to the current President Clinton scandal. At the time of this writing he was impeached by the house of representatives and is awaiting trial by the senate. The public is exposed to the same information yet people are divided in their support of the president. The majority support the president. What is interesting about those who support the president is that most are convinced by the allegations against the president regarding his immoral wrong doings, which include abuse of power, lying before a grand jury, perjury and subornation of justice. All of the latter pertain to his illicit sexual practices, including adultery with a number of women. Since most of the public has access to the same news and information by the major media, the question that arises is why is he so popular with the

---

27 The phenomenon of homeostasis relates to an equilibrium between emotions and behavior. Chapter 9, AGP Syndrome, will deal with this phenomenon in great detail.

majority of the public? His enemies are baffled and mystified about this.

The people are SELECTIVE about how they respond to the not-so-subtle, biased media. Those who support the president are aware of the power structure that controls the media. The application of selectivity is illustrated by the fact that notwithstanding their knowledge of the president's scandalous and immoral behavior, they continue to support the president. Many pundits of the media claim it is because of the country's good economic condition. But don't those of the public who want him out of the White House also know that? So why does one side SELECT one set of reasons for their decision, while the other side SELECTS another set of reasons when both sets of reasons are equally available to either side?

The complete answer is found not only in reality or logic, but also in unconscious predisposition. You must probe the unconscious for the complete answer. Those who support the president perceive the media and the power behind it, as trying to pressure them against their will to be against of the president. Many people react to the media with the same attitude they had had with their parents. Thus, the recalcitrant attitude towards their parents is projected on to the media. Then how does one explain those who side with the media and are against the president? Undoubtedly, they were 'good' children, submissive to their parents. As adults, they always conform to establishment. They are influenced by establishment and go along with the media as they did with their parents. There probably are other reasons why the public is divided, but in my opinion, the explanation given above is the main one. When there is unconscious motivation to defy authority, we simulate the hypnotic subject who opened the window.

Familiarity with the nature of posthypnotic suggestions helps us to understand neurotic symptoms. The latter are brought about as though it were the result of autosuggestion, motivated by the unconscious needs of an individual. Although one does not consciously use autosuggestion to bring about neurotic symptoms, the dynamics simulate auto-suggestion. The symptoms serve an important function in maintaining an individual's homeostasis.[28] The symptoms can be any one or combinations of either-or a variety of sensory and motor changes. I mentioned these changes above when discussing posthypnotic suggestion. Removal of a symptom by hypnosis without dealing with the fundamental neurotic need of that symptom upsets the existing homeostasis.[29] What follows is an experience at one of my seminars in hypnosis that illustrates the latter.

During a lecture on hypnosis I gave to a mixed group of dentists and physicians, I gave the reasons why hypnosis should not be used for symptom removal. I mentioned the most common neurotic symptoms for which patients come for treatment. Among the symptoms mentioned was stuttering. As usual, at the end of my lecture, individuals from the audience gathered around me to ask questions or discuss something. All departed except one physician. We were alone when he started with, "Dr Moss, I did not want to embarrass you during the lecture to tell you that you were wrong."

"About what?" I asked. He then told me that he was a stutterer and how he was cured by hypnosis.

"I signed up for six hypnotic sessions. The cure started at the third session. Now, as you can observe, I do not stutter any more." He was right. The stuttering was all gone. But I know with absolute certainty that another symptom has replaced the

---

28 This is amply documented in the psychoanalytic literature.

29 All RESPONSIBLE hypnotherapists know that the removal of a symptom by hypnosis, without dealing with the cause, results in another symptom that generally is more insidious than the one removed. Usually the subject remains oblivious of the connection

original one. When this happens the individual never connects the new symptom with the replaced symptom. I then took a 'shot in the dark' and asked him, "By the way, what happened to your sex life?" I hit a bull's eye. He reacted to my question with a staggering shock. He seemed to go into a stupor. The blood left his face blanched. Crestfallen, and without another word, he turned and walked away. It was obvious that he had become sexually impotent. The removal of his stuttering upset the home-ostasis that enabled him to be sexually potent. Until that moment he never connected his impotency with the removal of his stuttering.[30] The symptom, stuttering, produced by unconscious autosuggestion was removed without investigating and dealing with the unconscious function the symptom served. Removing the symptom did not remove the need. Successful analytic therapy removes the need for the symptom. The symptom leaves.

The next chapter will deal with symbolism, the language of the unconscious.

---

30 See Chapter 4, "Keep the Show on the Road."

CHAPTER 7

SYMBOLISM: THE LANGUAGE OF THE UNCONCIOUS

Wishes, emotions, conflicts, memories etc. that are either too threatening to cope with because of their forbidden nature, or too overwhelmingly painful, i.e., an ICR, are repressed from consciousness. They do not disappear from the mind but rather are stored away in the unconscious. Thus, you have no cognizance of their existence. Nature's censorship protects you from knowing or feeling the forbidden contents of the unconscious in order to enable you to function, i.e., "keep the show on the road."[31] The process of repression assuring survival starts early in life as part of the process of becoming 'humanized'.[32] Repression includes current ongoing reality and continues throughout life. With the passage of time there is a continuous build-up of stored repressed material concealed in the unconscious.

---

31 See Chapter 2, "Humanization of the Beast."
32 This is discussed in detail in chapter 10, "The Dream."

Some of what is in the unconscious is bursting at the periphery of the mind, i.e., the preconscious, attempting to erupt into consciousness. What keeps the contents of the unconscious from erupting into consciousness is our unconscious censor mechanism. Notwithstanding the latter, some material does erupts into consciousness during sleep when our intellect is not functioning and our defenses are down. Our dream material consists of that which was repressed and concealed in the unconscious. The censor continues to function since the dream material is so cleverly disguised that our dream cannot be identified with what is concealed in the unconscious. The disguise is a language of symbolism totally baffling to the intellect. Only by means of decoding the symbolic language can one arrive at the true meaning of the dream. What we remember of the dream is known as the MANIFEST content while that which is in the unconscious and hidden from us is known as the LATENT content. You arrive at the latent content, the true meaning of the dream, only when you decode the symbolic language.[33] The foregoing is an elementary explanation of the function of symbolism, e.g., how it conceals the contents of the unconscious from cognizance. What follow is an illustration that demonstrates the above.

Recall the spinster's reason for painting the bird at the museum.[34] Her reason was the beautiful bird set in a colorful landscape. But the real reason, motivated by her unconscious, was her sexuality. It was so couched in symbolism that she was unaware that the bird is a sexual symbol. In this way animals, inanimate objects, and even certain people become symbols or metaphors of one's aggression that often has a sexual basis. For

---

33 See Chapter 6.
34 Reichbart, Richard; *Heart Sybolism: Heart-Breast and Heart-Penis Equations*; The Psychoanalytic Review; Vol. 68:1; Spring, 1981 p. 71.

example, a person with an uncontrollable sexual drive, but over-whelmed with guilt about it, may repress it from consciousness. But in his/her dreams that person may identify with Marilyn Monroe, Mae West, Paul Newman and Robert Redford, President Clinton or Monica Lewinsky. All are sexual symbols that hide the truth about his/her own sexuality.

Since sexuality is so pervasive in our daily life, whether of not we are cognizant of it, there are a multitude of symbols regarding our sexuality. The sexual act may be symbolized by flying an airplane, electric current, an elevator, riding in a train, airplane, boat, underground, climbing, fighting, a vicious animal, walking in space, weightlessness and many dozens more. There is no limit to the number, character and nature of symbols. We unconsciously create symbols to represent the sex act or any aspect of sexuality. Thus, genitals may take on a multitude of symbolic representations. A penis could be a knife, gun, revolver, cannon, sword, telegraph pole, tree, broom, hammer, or any tool or piece of equipment. Any part of one's anatomy that projects may be a penis symbol(nose, ears and even tongue). Likewise, a female's genitals may be a cave or a house, or any body orifice such as mouth, rectum, and ears. A female may be symbolized as a kitchen because to some women the kitchen is identified with mother, wife, or feminism. Individuals and inanimate objects or animals may be symbols. The anus, rectum, buttocks, feces, the color black or brown (which may represent feces) may be symbols connoting homosexuality. There are an infinite number and varieties of symbolism dealing with any combination of our five senses.

Your own problems, wishes, fears or anxieties may be DISPLACED on an animal or on an inanimate object. An example of the former is dreaming about your cat's tumor which may be a symbol of your own fear of cancer. An example of an inanimate object as a symbol may be your soiled underwear which represents your 'dirty' thoughts about homosexuality. What follows are two quotes which indicate the typical kind of symbolism found in one's dreams and fantasies. Richard Reichbart describes the heart as follows,[35] "....because the heart has inherent characteristics, it plays a role in determining which objects or concepts are identified symbolically with the heart." The following are his reasons why the heart is chosen as symbol:[36]

1. The heart is the most vital organ of the body. Its proper functioning is a traditional sign of life; its failure to function is a traditional sign of death.
2. The heart is vulnerable to physical attack from the outside. When executed, there is an immediate collapse of the organ.
3. The heart is subject to dramatic and unexpected malfunctioning, which may be immediately fatal.
4. Because one can become aware of one's own heart or that of another person through the heartbeat; it is a unique organ of the body.
5. 1t is not within the conscious control of the individual.
6. It fluctuates greatly in conjunction with various emotions, internal and external stimuli, and physical and sexual functions.
7. The heart is situated beneath the breast of an individual.

Daniel Schneider, in his book, *The Image of the Heart* gives an in-depth analysis of the heart-related dreams and heart symptoms of his patients. He presents numerous instances of equations

---

35 ibid p.73
36 Schnieder, Danial; *The Image of the Heart*; International Press, N.Y. 1956, p. 62

such as heart=penis, heart=fetus, heart=child, heart=small, leaping animal, heart=clock, heart=hourglass. These equations combine with the heart=penis in the same manner as if A equals B; B equals C; then A equals C.[37]

In the first mentioned article Reichbarn equates the heart to the breast with the following explanation, "…I would suggest that the infant, who does not yet know the exact source of the mother's heartbeat, perceives itself as extension of the mother's breast…, as a consequence of these factors the heart eventually acquires an association to the warmth and tactile comfort of the breast's capacity to soothe the child when upset or frightened, and to the life sustaining mother's feeding of the infant. Substitution of heart for breast, as an object of oral aggression, is multi determined…"[38]

Symbolism is further complicated because of the fact that any or all the above symbols may be represented not as a whole but only a fragment of the whole, known as FRAGMENTATION. For example, a symbol of a disciplinarian parent may be a policeman, judge in a court of law, the President of the United States, etc. These symbols may be fragmented to represent a parent as a police badge, police club, black robe of a judge, a coin or dollar bill with an imprint of a president. The fragment then becomes a symbol of a symbol. Does that sound wacky? To the naive adult intellect it surely would. But to the unconscious it is everyday language. And when we learn how to decode that language, we discover meaning and order, rather than chaos, in the world of the unconscious.

---

37 ibid ref. #3 p. 76.
38 Freud, S.; *Three Contributions to the Sex Theory:* Trans. by Brill; Modern Library; NY, 1958, p.472.

INVERSION is another very important device for concealment. Everything is turned upside down or inside out. Very often what emerges into one's conscious awareness does so as an inverse reflection of the unconscious material. For example, an erotic wish may emerge as something repulsive. Sexual attraction for your sister-in-law may emerge as hate. Or the hatred of your sibling rival may emerge as love. Numerals may be reversed so that 51 may appear as 15. The unconscious employs any conceivable deception to prevent you from unmasking the disguise.

An individual having sex with his/her spouse may fantasize the vagina as: 1) his/her own rectum; 2) oral cavity of an infant at the mother's breast; 3) the oral cavity of a child receiving the father's penis. There are a multitude of combinations depending on the people in your life. Not only are personalities interchangeable, but so are the parts of their anatomy.[39] As already mentioned, any cavity of the body is interchangeable with the vagina, so, too, are all anatomical projections interchangeable as phallic symbols. For example, the penis may be the breasts, nose, tongue, etc. The testicles may be the breasts, ears or eyes. I make no attempt to list all possibilities. Bear in mind that whatever one perceives, regardless of its bizarre nature, originates from one's own imagination.

The image of yourself may be PROJECTED onto another person. The next chapter, *Fantasy Constellation* deals with this phenomenon.

---

39 Bollas, Christopher; *The Shadow of the Object*; Columbia University Press; NY, 1987. p.11.

CHAPTER 8

FANTASY CONSTELLATION

Although the professional literature does not mention the term FANTASY CONSTELLATION, there are frequent references to the concept. The constellations are unconscious fantasies in which you identify with another person. For example, you, the adult, may identify with your father and at the same time with the little boy/girl you once were. You may also identify with your little sister of age three and at the same time be the big brother/sister that you were at age five. You may be the little girl you were when playing with your doll, that may be yourself. Fantasy constellation occurs in dreams as well as on the analytic couch. Christopher Bolas says, "At any moment in an analytic session, a patient could be speaking through the voice of the mother, or some fragmented voice of father."[40] Familiarity with the concept of fantasy constellation can serve as a key to help decode symbolism, a prerequisite to dream interpretation.

---

40 If this seems too difficult to accept, I suggest that you reread Chapter 2, "The Magical Power of the Unconscious," to understand the magical nature of the unconscious.

Understanding and applying the concept of fantasy constellation in your analytic sessions can be a very useful, not only in your professional practice but also in your own personal life. Many disciplinarian problems that a parent has with his/her child can be understood and managed if the parent, (who may be yourself) is helped to gain insight relative to the concept of fantasy constellation. In fantasizing the role of both your parent and yourself, the child, you are continuing the job of the disciplining parent. Specifically, you are punishing yourself to eliminate the residual 'badness' that you continue to harbor in your own unconscious. (My colleagues, you must never forget that for the rest of your lives, you will always be the child you once were. If, in your training analysis you were not convinced of this, it is my opinion that your training was faulted.) I have helped therapists who were my patients, to vastly improve their relationship with their own children after they gained insight relative to the foregoing. You also will be a better therapist if you apply the foregoing to your patients.

Fantasy life already exists at the time of birth. Then, for a period of time after birth, the infant's world consists only of the mother. Later it extends to other family members, the father and/or siblings. Thus, the fantasy life of an infant can originate only from the world it has experienced, the world of parents and siblings. Throughout life, there is always the tendency to create fantasy constellations with all the people to whom we relate. All of such constellations are based on two archetypes. The first is the CHILD-PARENT; the second, CHILD-CHILD.

ARCHETYPE ONE. Child-Parent: A child often imagines itself to be the mother or father in its fantasies when at play or other activities. The sex of the parents is interchangeable in this fantasy world. Sometimes the child fantasizes itself as an aunt/ uncle, policeman, judge, teacher, military general, president of a country, employer, bishop or pope. or any other authority figure. This is often observed in games children play. Frequently adults have fantasies of being their own child. Children may fantasize a constellation in which they take on an adult role. For example, a boy may fantasize that he is his own father, having sex with his mother—heterosexual constellation; or that same boy, at another time, may fantasize himself replacing his mother, having sex with his own father—homosexual constellation.

What follows is the case of MB to illustrate ARCHETYPE ONE, CHILD-PARENT: MB, a female CEO in a prestigious, Madison Avenue, public relations firm, phoned me at my home, six thirty in the morning pleading for an emergency appointment.— Shehad been my patient and had quit treatment after several months—She sounded very distressed. I rearranged my schedule to see her. She was very distraught. She started immediately with: "Yesterday I had a distressing altercation with a subordinate female worker. I decided to discharge her, a decision about which I felt very guilty. Upon leaving my office and arriving at the garage where my car was parked, I could not find my car keys. I searched my briefcase and my large shoulder bag. It was in vain. The parking attendant called the police to break into my car. This was a mess that intensified my already great distressed state. Before going to bed that night, I went on a binge and raided the refrigerator." MB, a slightly overweight person, was disciplined about her diet. "With the discomfort of a stuffed stomach, I tossed and turned for hours before I fell asleep." After a brief pause she continued, "I had a frightening dream. I was being chased by a woman. I ran and ran but could not escape from her pursuit. There was much more, but I can't remember what it was."

What emerged during that one analytic session was that she discharged one of her female empoyees. In so doing she fantasized herself to be both her mother punishing herself, the little girl she once was. Her distress vacillated between the little girl's hatred of the mother and the guilt of the mother for punishing her child.[41] All parents feel guilty when they punish their child.[42]

ARCHETYPE TWO. These are fantasies that deal with a child's competitiveness with siblings in school or with competition among employees on the job. Another example is a student striving for a teacher's attention and interest, in competition with other students. This rivalry archetype exists even when there is no sibling. The child is in competition with one parent to get the love of the other. The competition between the mother and daughter for the husband's/father's love also is a variation of archetype two. The latter applies the same way with a son's competition with his father for the mother's love.

The case of Little Joey, described in chapter two, is an example of archetype two.[43] From the moment Joey's rival became a part of the family, his life changed. Joey will be coping with this problem when in school in competition with other students in his class; when playing little league baseball; in the office on the job in competition with others seeking a promotion; and when becoming a candidate for president of The United States. Fantasy constellation is chiseled into our psyche and remains there forever.

From moment to moment, we can instantaneously drift from the world of reality to the world of fantasy, or from one archetype to another. A common example of the latter is a man in the

---

41 The case of MB involves the AGP SYNDROME. This will be discussed in the next chapter and in the last chapter dealing with what to look for that is concealed in the unconscious.

42 See Chapter 4, "Keep the Show on the Road."

43 This experience is not as common among younger adults when the biological sex drive is strong enough to overcome most obstacles. Its occurrence after the age of fifty is much more common.

act of sexual intercourse with a woman. He may have a 'willing', tumescent, throbbing penis, well on the way toward consummation of the sexual act. Then, without warning, the penis goes limp and useless as a sexual organ. The sudden distressing change follows a disparaging remark make by his partner, such as: "Don't touch me there, it hurts; I don't want you to kiss me because you have halitosis; Your beard is like sandpaper, I can't stand it." Such critical remarks sometimes can spark a child-parent fantasy. The critical partner becomes the disciplinarian mother; the man, the impotent infant.[44]

There are a multitude of fantasy constellations in regards to sexuality. The bizarre and 'magical' unconscious uses various constellations according to the level of one's regression, i.e., pre-Oedipal or post-Oedipal.[45] The pre-Oedipal level involves symbolism that relates to the oral cavity and/or the anus. The oral cavity represents the vagina; the penis the mother's breast. The post-Oedipal involves symbolism related to the genital organs. The symbolism may treat the vagina as though it were the rectum. It could ba your own rectum: 1) during infancy; 2) during childhood, 3) during adolescence; 4) your current life; 5) the rectum of either of your parents. The foregoing is the explanation why some individuals have a predilection for oral sex, for anal sex, fellatio, cunnilingus or any imaginable sexual variation.

For those who find the foregoing incredible, consider that in the small country of Nepal, in the Himalayan mountains, the most sacred religious symbol inside the temples of worship is that of the canine animal with a penis many feet long. It is wrapped around the female human figure. It enters her vagina

---

44 Salzman, Leon: Discussion on the Freudean concept of Infantile Sexuality; Modern Psychoanalysis; Basic Books; 1968 p. 126.
45 Han, Suyan; *The Mountain is Young*; Putman Pub. Co.; NY, 1958.

or rectum and emerges through the oral cavity. There are numerous such symbols in the form of magnificent statues, frescos and paintings on the walls of these temples-Until the past several decades, foreigners were forbidden entrance to the temples, but it has been done illicitly.[46] [47]

Pornographic literature is replete with fanciful, creative varieties of fantasy constellations. Hermann Hesse, the deceased German novelist, used the metaphor for fantasy constellation in his novel Steppenwolf.[48] Although Hesse never expressed his concept as fantasy constellation, it is an excellent artist's understanding of the phenomenon. Harry, the main character, was given 35 dolls, which represented anyone in Harry's life. He was given the power to arrange them in any relationship he wished; the role of mother, father, little brother/sister, big brother/sister, one's doll, teddy bear, teacher, soldier, policeman, etc. In each case a slightly different constellation occurs with Hesse's 35 dolls. The understanding of the phenomenon of fantasy constellation opens up significant possibilities in decoding symbolism. It is applied in the last step of the Moss Method.

The next chapter deals with the very important concept known as the Aggression-Guilt-Punishment syndrome (AGP).

---

46 Rushbrook, Wm.; *Travelers in India, Pakistan and Sri Lanka*; Facts Pub. Co; NY; 1982

47 Hesse, Hermann; *Steppenwolf*; (Henry Holt Pub. Co., 1957).

48 Freedman, Lawrence Z.; *Psychoanalysis, Delinquency and the Law*; Basic Books, 1968, p. 654.

CHAPTER 9

THE AGP SYNDROME

This chapter is one of the two most important chapters. The other is the last chapter that deals with the practical procedures of the Moss Method for Self-analysis.

About twenty-five years ago, after many years of self-analysis, I made the important discovery of the AGP (**A**ggression-**G**uilt-**P**unishment) syndrome. I am amazed that up to now no one has come forth with the concept of the AGP syndrome, so simple and yet so profound. In some aspects, it is similar to Freud's Id-Superego-Ego concept, but it is not the same. The difference will be born out as this chapter unfolds. I strongly believe that applying the AGP syndrome opens up vast therapeutic possibilities both for dyadic analysis and for self-analysis. Its proper application can drastically shortcut the time for analytic treatment by months or even years. It is particularly useful in self-analysis because knowing what to look for, namely the AGP syndrome, overcomes some of the subjectivity that many believe is an obstacle to self-analysis. The practical procedure of how the AGP syndrome applies to self-analysis will be described in great detail in Chapters 15 and 16.

The AGP syndrome is a homeostatic relationship between one's aggression, guilt and the punishment. It starts to take shape at birth. By the time one reaches the tender age of five, it already is well established. It remains as a vital force until death.

What follows is a description of each of the three elements of the AGP syndrome as they are perceived by the unconscious:

1) *AGGRESSION* Your unconscious perceives aggression quite differently from how your conscious does. Aggression may be something in one's overt reality (conscious and/or voluntary) or in the realm of fantasy. The unconscious reacts the same to either, since the unconscious does not distinguish reality from fantasy. For schematic purposes, I classify aggression into four categories as it relates to the AGP syndrome: 1) PARENTAL DEFIANCE, 2) SEXUAL, 3) BEHAVIORAL, 4) EMOTIONAL EXPRESSION.

1) PARENTAL DEFIANCE. Defiance against the parents is the most primitive and earliest form of aggression. Because to the infant/child the parents are omnipotent and omniscient, it is the most extreme form of aggression, punishable by annihilation.

2) SEXUAL. Sexuality, overt as well as fantasy, is perceived by the unconscious as aggression. All forms of creativity derive their force from the sexual drive. Thus, composing a symphony, writing a book or a poem, acting or participation in theater, creative science or mathematics, surgery that is creatively done for the first time, etc. is sublimation of one's sexual drive.[49]

3) BEHAVIORAL. Much of what are considered normal activities may be *perceived by the unconscious* as aggression. Competitiveness in school, on the workplace, one's profession (law, medicine,

---

49 Hall, Calvin, S.; Primer of Freudian Psychology, New American Library; 1985, p. 116

clergy, teachers and educators, science) sports, gambling in the stock market or race track, getting ahead on the job, etc. is perceived by the unconscious as aggressions are rebellion against acceptable conventions in clothes, body piercing—so widespread among our youth—issues of morality and/or ethics; cheating on income tax, etc. I stress the importance of the difference of how the unconscious perceives aggression compared to how it is perceived by the intellect.

4) EMOTIONAL EXPRESSION. Other examples of aggression are such emotions as hostility, envy, jealousy, selfishness, etc. Our culture treats these emotions as 'bad'. We are often reprimanded or punished for such forbidden emotions.

The foregoing are only a few examples to illustrate how ubiquitous the unconscious perceives aggression *as it relates to the AGP syndrome*. To underscore what was mentioned above I repeat, aggression need not be in the form of overt behavior. It exists also in the realm of fantasies, some of which never reach consciousness, e.g., in our dreams, of which we are unaware because it is shrouded in symbolism. The latter will be discussed in the next chapter dealing with dreams and in the last chapter dealing with analytic interpretation.

2). *Guilt.* Aggression cannot exist without the consequence of guilt. Guilt starts to develop early in infancy resulting from the disciplinary process. Any item in the above list of aggressive behavior or fantasies may produce guilt in some individuals varying from mild to extreme. Not all guilt is consciously experienced since it emerges only in our dreams. We all experience some degree of guilt for behavior that is illegal, culturally taboo or forbidden even though it is not cognizant. However, I have encountered individuals who are totally devoid of any conscious feelings of guilt. For them guilt is too threatening for their weak egos to deal with. Their defenses keep guilt from reaching consciousness. But the repressed guilt in such individuals not only emerges in their dreams but also may result in neurotic, conversion symptoms and/or behavior aberrations. This is frequently true of sexual guilt. Because of the persuasiveness of unconscious guilt, whatever guilt emerges into consciousness is only a tiny part of what is concealed in our unconscious.

3) PUNISHMENT. The acculturation of the infant necessitates discipline by authority starting with the parents, educational and religious institutions, governments with its law and order establishments. Discipline of the infant/child is based on the use of reward and punishment. The latter consists of many forms, some of which may be obvious, while others are subtle and not so obvious. Children have a heightened capacity to perceive punishment, even in its most subtle form. Only weeks after birth, the infant is capable of preverbal communication. The perceptive mother can discern the infant's message by the nature of its cry. The infant is affected by an offensive grimace, the quality of its mother's voice, a smile, a kiss, a hug all of which is either reward of love and acceptance. The infant reads facial expression showing dissatisfaction, frustration, anger all of which is equated to punishment. In passing from infancy to childhood, one becomes aware which of their aggressive acts and thoughts are acceptable and which forbidden. The latter when acted out by the child produce guilt for which the child may be reprimanded or punished.

Punishment cancels out the guilt, thereby establishing homeostasis. This concept is applied to the criminal who pays for his crime with a fine and/or prison sentence and is then free. Without punishment, or the threat of punishment, the beast within us is released not only in the child but also in the adult. We are all familiar with the rape and pillage that breaks loose when victorious armies enter and occupy the territory of a defeated enemy; or how vandalism, stealing and rioting take place when a catastrophe strikes and there is no authority present.

Children unconsciously provoke punishment. It is recurrent pattern of behavior that sets limits to the boundaries of the child's aggression. After the child is punished, it is well behaved and 'good' for a period of days or weeks, at which time it again pushes beyond the limits of acceptable behavior. It must again be punished. The time interval of the cycle between aggression, guilt and punishment varies from child to child. It is claimed that the child needs the punishment in order to establish the limits of acceptable behavior. Most authorities are aware of the child's need for punishment. Awareness of this need is what motivates the saying "spare the rod and spoil the child." This is not to imply that I recommend punishment. But among those who do, there is the premise that because limits are set by punishment, the child thereby feels more secure. I reject this belief out-of-hand.

The need for punishment and suffering, which is well-rooted in early childhood, stays with you for the rest of your life. Since you never cease to be a child, you never overcome the need of punishment. "Punishment for what?" you may ask. The answer is, unconscious guilt based on repressed aggression. Our animalistic instincts never cease to collide with our culture. Thus, pervasive guilt is present in all of us at all times. The frivolous saying, "Everything in life that gives joy and/or pleasure is either illegal, immoral or fattening," has a deep and serious portent.

Each child is unique in regard to how much guilt and how much punishment is necessary to control his/her aggression. To one child, a mild scolding might have a more profound effect than another child who is physically beaten. Some can cope with more guilt than others. We develop an equilibrium between our aggression, our guilt and the need for punishment. PUNISHMENT

CANCELS OUT THE GUILT, thereby reestablishing one's homeostasis. Each individual has his/her own particular balance about the amount of aggression, guilt and punishment that constitute that individual's homeostasis.

Disturbances of homeostasis occur in our dreams when our defenses are down. Our aggressive fantasies are out of control when we sleep, often running wild and amok. This results in our AGP getting out of balance. These uncontrollable fantasies produce guilt, which in turn necessitates punishment to reestablish homeostasis. A frightening dream should be dealt with as punishment. When we awaken from a frightening dream, or sometimes a nightmare, we often forget the aggression and guilt; we remember only the punishment component of the AGP triad. Even though we do not recall the aggression and the guilt, we know it exists because one component of the AGP syndrome cannot exist by itself. Thus, we search for the other two components. Recall the case of MB discussed in chapters 8 and 9. All she remembered of her dream was the terror of being chased. That was punishment. Her aggression, the discharge of her employee, i.e., taking on the role of her mother punishing the child, i.e., herself, and the guilt associated with that aggression was completely repressed from her dream. Taking on the role of the mother also had a sexual connotation, one that produces intense guilt. She replaced her mother in bed with her father. Most sexual fantasies often result in nightmares in individuals who are sexually maladjusted.[50] The need for punishment for taking on the role of mother was the reason she could not find her keys. If she didn't have the need for punishment, she would have found her keys in the bottom of her shoulder bag. She

---

50 A Big Affair; TV WNET; April 22, 1989.

discovered her keys only after she arrived home, at which time she was more thorough in her search.

In the neurotic individual or during periods of emotional distress there is an imbalance in the relationship of the three components of the triad. The homeostasis is upset when the AGP forces are out of balance. It results in distressful changes, such as over- anxiety, depression accompanied by a masochistic need for punishment. MB's guilt upset her homeostasis and threw her AGP out of balance. Her need for punishment reestablished her homeostasis. Later in this chapter, I shall cite a number of examples of the need for punishment because of the disturbed homeostasis.

No one is free of guilt. It varies in quality and quantity according to the individual's tolerance. Because of ubiquitous guilt, the unconscious tends to perceive every traumatic experience or mishap and the suffering that result, as punishment. At times one feels irrationally responsible for a totally irrelevant and uncontrollable event for which one is being punished. The following is an example that was shown in a TV movie:[51] The parents of a six-year-old girl had just separated, considering divorce. The child who remained with her mother kept promising over and over again, "I'll eat my cereal every morning if daddy would come home." Because of the need for punishment (unconscious, of course), the suffering is often greatly intensified, totally out of proportion to the mishap or circumstances. Much unnecessary suffering is the result of the irrational perception that a mishap or traumatic event is punishment for that ever constant, unconscious guilt. Examples of suffering that the conscious perceives as punishment are the loss of a loved one, serious accidents resulting in the loss of a limb; serious illness such as cancer; catastrophic financial losses, etc. Such individuals keeps asking,

---

51 The time of writing this is December, 1998

"Why me, why me?" They often search for their aggressive misdeed or bad behavior, past or present. A fifty year old individual may feel he/she is being punished for his/her sexual promiscuity of twenty years ago.

When the unconscious need for punishment and suffering impacts on our lives, there is an unconscious compulsion to become careless or negligent in order to make mistakes that result in suffering. We react to this suffering as though it were punishment. Punishment for what? Some aggressive act that produced guilt. All of this, of course, is an unconscious phenomenon. We act as though we were hypnotized not to use our heads. Over the years, I have made mistakes, which could have been avoided if I had used my head. The latter caused me agonizing pain and suffering. I have found the 'mistake-accident' phenomenon in every patient that I have treated. You, the therapist, will also discover the mistake-accident phenomenon in yourself and in your patients, if you look for it. It is there!

In the previous chapter, "Fantasy Constellation", the case of MB, exhibited all of the salient features of the AGP syndrome: her aggression in discharging an employee, her guilt, and her need for punishment. Losing her keys and the distress that followed were punishment that she brought to herself. If she had been more careful in searching her shoulder bag, she would have found her keys and would have avoided the painful consequences. She did not use her head because of her need for punishment.

What now follows are eight cases, taken from my files—plus a ninth case, just added, the President Clinton scandal[52]—of individuals who like MB, 'did not use their head.' These cases are selected to show how pervasivenss AGP syndrome exists in our daily lives. In each of the cases, aggressive behavior resulted in

---

52 Cheating on tax returns is a very common form of aggression.

guilt necessitating punishment in order to reestablish the homeostasis. I stress the fact that the entire process is an unconscious phenomenon.

1. John usually commuted to work by train from Westchester to Grand Central Station, New York. Then he subways to his office located in the Manhattan Wall Street area. One day John drove his auto to work because he had to bring a bulky package to his office. At the end of a strenuous day, before picking up his car on a parking lot, John stopped at a bar for a drink to "loosen up". Just as he was about to leave, a friend, whom he hadn't seen for a long time, entered the bar. He had a second drink for old time's sake. Forgetting that he had over an hour's drive to get home he took a third drink. In his slightly inebriated state he drove faster than usual to make up for the lost time because he remembered that several days before, his wife made a dinner engagement with some friends. He never arrived home that evening. Instead he ended up in the hospital with a fractured jaw, leg and arm. Months later when he was in therapy with me what emerged was that John was having an affair with his secretary. The guilt resulting from his sexual aggression necessitated punishment to reestablish his homeostasis. This could have been prevented *if he had used his head.*

2. Dennis was in bed with a slight fever. He was a victim of a flu epidemic. After six days the fever broke. In spite of the fact that he still felt weak, and that his doctor warned him to stay indoors for 24 to 48 hours after he was free of the fever, he went out into the night air the day his fever broke. He and his wife had tickets to a Broadway show. He arrived home feverish and with a splitting headache. He spent the next two weeks bedridden with a fever gyrating daily from 101 to 103. His convalescence lasted a whole month. Months later, when in therapy, he revealed that he had just put his protesting mother into a nursing home.

He was riddled with guilt. The guilt demanded punishment to reestablish his homeostasis. This could have been prevented *if he had used his head.*

3. Jim loaned $1,800.00 to George, a co-worker, who pleaded that he needed the money to pay for his wife's operation. Jim knew that George was a gambler and a deadbeat. But Jim believed George when he promised full payment within a month. After 6 months and several broken promises, George lost his job. He never paid back the loan. "I hated myself for my stupidity. I gave myself a good kick in the pants," he grumbled during an analytic session. What emerged was that Jim experienced guilt for getting a promotion that bypassed George. The situation involved unresolved, sibling rivalry. His unconscious hostility towards his rival was repressed aggression. His aggression, although unconscious, brought on guilt that necessitated punishment to reestablish his homeostasis. This could have been prevented *if he had used his head.*

4. Jack was chopping some firewood in the backyard of his country home. He held the wood with one hand and swung the ax with the other. He miscalculated and chopped off the ends of two fingers. This could have been prevented *if he had used his head.* In therapy it was revealed that he had guilt resulting from a phone confrontation with his daughter who was attending an out-of-town college. She was disappointed that he did not buy her an auto as he promised he would. He tried to explain to his daughter that because his business took a downward turn, he could not afford that 'luxury'. She claimed it was a necessity. They argued. When in therapy, he revealed that he experienced oppressive guilt for breaking his promise. The guilt demanded punishment to reestablish his homeostasis. He was careless. This could have been prevented *if he had used his head*

5. Jerry climbed up a ladder to the second floor on the outside of his home to install a summer window screen. Because the ladder was not properly secured it slipped and Jerry fell to the ground. He ended up in the hospital with a broken hip bone. In his therapy, Jerry discussed his intention to terminate his sixteen-year marriage. "My wife, whom I was deserting for another woman, had developed multiple sclerosis," he painfully revealed. He was in great conflict, suffering extreme guilt. The suffering from the accident was the punishment that reestablished his homeostasis. This could have been avoided *if he had used his head*.

6. Danny was happily married. He was attending an-out of-town convention. He had sex with a hooker, whom he picked up at the hotel bar where he was staying. The hooker assured him that she was clean; that he needn't bother about a condom. Because he believed her, he came down several days later with a severe case of gonorrhea. The guilt for cheating on his wife needed punishment. This could have been prevented *if he had used his head*.

7. Mary, a housewife, struck a match and was about to light the oven. Just then, the telephone rang. Before she answered the phone, she snuffed out the flame on the match, but she forgot to turn off the open gas jet. She came back a few minutes later, lit another match and opened the oven. The explosion that followed cost Mary weeks in the hospital with burns over her face and neck. In therapy she revealed that for weeks before the accident, Mary experienced endless guilt for denying sex to her husband. This could have been prevented *if she had used her head*.

8. Louise, an experienced driver, on her way to her country home, passed a car on a curve of a two-lane highway. She collided with an oncoming car. She was hospitalized for five weeks with internal and spinal injuries. The driver of the other car was killed. Louise's tax returns were under investigation by the IRS for

fraud.[53] She was wrought up with guilt and fear. This accident could have been prevented *if she had used her head.*

William Jefferson Clinton baffles the pundits of our media. They are mystified why such a brilliant individual was so stupid to bring all the suffering on to himself. If they were familiar with the AGP phenomenon they would know the answer. Because our president was born and raised in a Judeo-Christian culture he must have been overwhelmed with unbearable guilt for his sexual transgressions. Although the guilt may not have been conscious during his sexual escapades, one can assume with one hundred percent certainty that it permeated his unconscious. His public admissions of remorse and his pleading for forgiveness is evidence that he now is overwhelmed with conscious guilt. How great his unconscious need for punishment must have been to bring all this disgrace and agony on to himself. The pundits need look no further to solve the enigma. President Clinton could have been avoided this disastrous debacle *if he had used his head.*

The common denominator of all the above cases is *out-of-control aggression.* This resulted in the disruption of AGP homeostasis. If you would contend that these cases were everyday occurrences that could have happened to any of us, I would heartily agree. To one degree or another, we all harbor unconscious guilt. If the guilt of your aggression in your overt life is repressed, as probably was the case with President Clinton, and if the aggression is out of control, there is trouble ahead. The impact of the unconscious on your behavior and perception, is to act as though you were hypnotized not to use your head. You then do stupid things that result in punishment needed to reestablish your homeostasis

---

53 Freud, S.; *On Dreams*; Collected Works; Standard Ed., Vol. 5; Hogarth Press; London, 1953, p. 482.

In this chapter I tried to indicate the following: 1) pervasiveness of the AGP syndrome. 2) the relationship between the AGP syndrome and homeostasis that exists in each of us. 3) Everything that we do or think, invested with emotion, has one or more component of the AGP syndrome. Thus, searching for the AGP phenomenon is a valuable aid in psychoanalysis, both in dyadic-analysis and in self-analysis. It gives one a clue of what to search for. This will be discussed in great detail in the last chapter.

I want to close this chapter with an admonition: "Never forget that the unconscious has the magical power to convert a tiny mole hill (any one of the three components of the AGP syndrome) into a huge mountain."

The dream phenomenon will be discussed in the next chapter.

Section two

(Practical)

CHAPTER 10

THE DREAM: Part 1

This chapter deals with the theoretical aspects of the dream. The next chapter, "The Dream, Part 2," will deal with the practical application of the dream to the Moss Method for Self-analysis.

What is a dream? Why does one dream? Does the dream serve any purpose? What makes one dream? Why do some people dream while others do not? These are some of the questions with which this chapter deals. Although dreams deal with the past, present and the future, no analyst will agree with those who believe that dreams are clairvoyant and can predict the future

The dream is an eruption of something in the unconscious, e.g., emotions, conflicts, memories, etc., that are repressed. The analyst's object is to help the patient to cope with repressed material because the latter often impacts harmfully on his/her life resulting in compulsive and/or irrational behavior and/or neurotic symptoms.

Does eruption of something from the unconscious mean that nature's censorship has failed us? Absolutely not. Nature continues to conceal from us whatever was repressed by disguising the erupted material in symbolism. In this way the dream reveals none of the secrets in the unconscious. The dream that emerges and erupts into consciousness upon awakening is known as the MANIFEST content. That which is concealed from awareness, the real and deeper meaning, is known as the LATENT content.

According to most authorities dreaming occurs with great regularity in all human beings of all ages. Freud, the most prominent authority on dreams, made the statement so popular among psychoanalysts, "The interpretation of a dream is the royal road to the knowledge of the unconscious activities of the mind,"[54] implying that through the interpretation of the dream can we arrive at its latent content The meaning and interpretation of dreams vary with the different schools of psychotherapy. Three examples follow: 1) Karen Horney states, "In dreams we are closer to the reality of ourselves; they represent attempts to solve our conflicts, either in a neurotic or in a healthy way; that in them constructive forces could be at work, even at a time that they are hardly visible otherwise."[55] 2) Anthony Storr says, "Dreams may contain ineluctable truths, philosophical pronouncements, illusions, wild fantasies, memories, plans, anticipations, irrational experiences, even telepathic visions, and heaven knows what besides."[56] 3) One of Freud's views was, "People who have been subjected to some 'traumatic incident' may have recurrent dreams in which the incident occurs undisguised. Freud postulated that the dream was an attempt at mastering a disturbing incident.[57]

---

54 Storr, Anthony, The Art of Psychotherapy; Routledge Pub. NY, 1990, p.46.

55 Storr, Anthony, The Art of Psychotherapy; Routledge Pub. NY, 1990, p.46.

56 Jones, Ernest; Sigmond Freud; Vol. 1, Hogarth Press, 1953, p.268.

57 ibid ref. #4, p.38.

The dream reorganizes the reality by modifying it in one or a combination of the following four ways: 1) condensation, the fusing together of different ideas and/or images into a single image; 2) Displacement, in which a potentially disturbing image or idea is replaced by something less disturbing; 3) Representation, The process by which thoughts are converted into visual images; and 4) symbolization, in which some neutral objects stand for, or allude to, some aspects of sexual life and/or alludes to those persons connected with it which the dreamer would prefer not to recognize.[58]

The following is a list of ways in which a dream may be emerge:

I) A dream may be a simple event that consists of one or more parts. The parts may or may not be related. When they are not related the connection can be made only by the analytic process.

2) There may be more than one dream and at times as many as five or more, simultaneously.

3) The dream may emerge as only a sentence or a statement of some sort, even though you may remember that there was more.

4) It may be a name or a bizarre, nonexistent word, or a melody. Any of these bits may linger on for hours, or may be forgotten, then may be remembered later on during the day. What is even more bizarre is that any of the bits described above, or even a single word repeating itself over and over again, may be all that is remembered. Any of the bits remembered are important because they may be the key to an entire dream. The technique of how to apply the key to recover the main body of the dream will be dealt with in the last of the six steps of the Moss Method.

5) A dream may be a picture or a bizarre sound or just about anything conceivable by unbridled imagination. New words are often invented and may be the only thing remembered about a

---

58 Jong, Erica; *Fear of Flying*; Holt, Rinehart and Winston; NY.,1973.

dream. The entire dream is often a metaphor disguised in symbolism, so that the unknown latent content of the dream remains concealed until decoded or analyzed. In this way the dream reveals none of the secrets of the unconscious.

Dreams fall into two categories: 1) A recurring dream, one that keeps repeating itself at daily, weekly, or monthly intervals. 2) A non-recurrent dream that has nothing that relates to any previous dreams.

What follows is a list of recurrent dreams, most of which are my own.

1) The death of a family member or friend. In the dream the dead person is alive and well and may even be engaged in a conversation with you. The dream represents your inability to deal with the void resulting from the death. This is especially true during the first year after the death of a spouse, parent, child or loved one. These recurrent dreams, in which dead people are alive, are sometimes so real that you are often bewildered upon awakening to discover that it was only a dream. The explanation is that although the conscious intellect accepts and deals with the reality, the unconscious does not. In chapter two, I emphasized the magical nature of the unconscious mind. The dead come back to life; magic prevails.

2) Dreams that recreate a marital relationship even of one who may have been divorced months or years.

3) A variation of this theme for one who gave up smoking, but in the dream continues to smoke, as in the past. The dreamer wonders, even in the dream, "when did I commence to smoke?" What a relief to wake up and to discover it was only a dream. This applies to any and all past drug addictions.

4) One may have lost a limb or body member, but that in the dream is present and continues to function. Here again the unconscious refuses to accept the reality and resorts to magic.

5) Sexual dream: You are engaged in lovemaking and are about to climax, but you awaken, frustrated and disappointed. This may represent a frustration in your life that may be non-sexual in nature. You already are in your middle forties and are disappointed or unhappy about your status or attainment of your goal towards 'success', a reality that you are unable to deal with. Repressing this reality simply transfers the frustration to the unconscious where it is converted into sexual failure and frustration.

6) Regression back to school. You are perplexed even in the dream because you know that you have completed your schooling and are already practicing your profession or occupation. A variation of this dream is to be late or unprepared for an exam; or unable to find your classroom.

7) Driving an auto or any other vehicle and losing control of the brakes when trying to avoid a collision. This dream represents the anxiety of losing control of your aggression. The collision may be the punishment component of the AGP syndrome.

8) Flying or walking in space. This represents fulfillment of sexual aggression. This anxiety is obvious in the title of Erica Jung's novel "The Fear Of Flying."[59] What one dare not experience in real life, one often experiences in fantasy life, the dream.

9) Falling through space is to reexperience the most primitive fear of the helpless infant. It is a punishment type of dream.[60]

---

59 You must always presume that aggression and guilt is related to every punishment dream.

60 It is a common occurrence that when a man is traumatized by a major mishap—loss of any of the following: eyesight, limb, financial fortune,—he may become impotent. It may be temporary, if it occurs below the age of forty to fifties. Analytic therapy is often effective for recovery.

There are many other varieties of common dreams, some of which are recurrent. Each person is a creator of dreams with no limits to his/her imagination. I discovered that almost all dreams contain one or more of the components of the AGP syndrome. I consider this an important breakthrough in dream analysis. Applying the AGP concept in dream analysis is a powerful tool both in dyadic analysis and in self-analysis. It may be a wedge that opens doors to the unconscious. One or more of the three components could be found in most of our dreams. Therefore, searching for the component in dreams of my own and of my patients, has became a routine procedure. This is readily confirmed by those analysts whom I have taught to use this tool. A detailed explanation of how this is done is discussed in Chapters 15 and 16, when the practical procedure of analytic interpretation is dealt with.

What now follows is a case taken from my files that displays many of the phenomena described in this chapter and in all the preceding chapters.

The case of S.D. A fifty-five year old man had been my next door neighbor in a motel complex in upstate New York, in the Lake Champlain area. After becoming acquainted, we decided to hire a boat and go fishing. It was in this tranquil lake setting that I told him that I was a psychotherapist. Knowing this, he wondered whether I could tell him the meaning of a recurrent dream that vexed him. Since S.D. was naive about such things, I explained to him that I would not be able to analyze his dream, but if he told me his dream, I might be able to give him an idea about what the dream deals with. The following is what he told me:

"I am erecting a fence in the front of my home separating the sidewalk from the front lawn. The fence would be about 100 feet long. I dug holes into the ground at 10 foot intervals with the intention of sinking posts into each hole. I would then have upper and lower parallel logs connecting the post. This is a common type of fence in the neighborhood where I live. After all the 10 holes were completed, I started to place a post in each hole. I already have four posts in position. But something always happens with the *fifth one*. The post is so heavy that I am barely able to lift the post; but when I did, *I just couldn't get it into the hole*. It is as though there was some force that kept repelling it away. I am perplexed, distressed and frustrated about my failure. My wife occasionally appears in the dream trying to help me to *insert the pole*. She also is disappointed. I have to give up the project of erecting the fence". [italics mine]

"Did you say that this is a recurrent dream?" 1 asked.

"Yes, different aspects come to me from time to time. In some dreams, I am digging the holes only, while in other dreams, I am wrestling with the post. Then at other times, I am very apologetic to my wife about my failure. Could you tell me what this is all about?"

"In a general way, I could characterize your dream as one dealing with sex," I told him, "but to actually analyze the dream I would have to know much more about your personal and private life."

"Oh, you are quite wrong," he came back at me. "The fact is that I have had no desire for sex for the past five years. I lost all interest in sex."

Gliding along Lake Champlain on a lazy summer day, I had enough leisure time to explain the nature of dreams. He was both fascinated and surprised at my explanation. I pointed out to him the various sexual symbols. Though they may be blatantly obvious to the informed reader, nevertheless, they were unknown to S.D. Fortunately, he was open-minded respecting my knowledge in these matters. Therefore, it was relatively easy for me to convince him that his dream was heavily invested with sexuality. He then revealed the details of a trauma that occurred in his life about five years previously.

At age forty-five I became an entrepreneur. I took over the auto sales agency that employed me and six others. It was an ambitious goal on my part, but it always was my dream and desire to own my own business. I had been a auto salesman up to then, and I was convinced that it is 'now or never' for me to make it big. I used all my savings, plus whatever I could borrow from my friends and family. I went into hock. My calculations were poor and after a year or so I went bankrupt and lost everything. I needn't tell you what a trauma this was. I was depressed for many months before I could pull myself together. My wife supported me and made it possible for me, at age fifty, to pick up my life and resume my job as a salesman. That's how I earn my livelihood today. I'm getting by O.K.; but with shattered illusions of ever getting rich.

During the period of my depression I made a number of attempts at intercourse with my wife; but they were always unsuccessful. I, who had a good sex life, was now impotent. This made me feel even worse. I finally stopped trying. Every now and then my wife cuddles up to me, hoping that something in me would be stirred up. But when I try, it is always the same. I can't get an erection. I feel guilty about failing my wife, who is now only in her middle forties."

S.D. subsequently became my patient.

There could be no doubt that the post and hole in the ground symbolically represented penis and vagina, respectively. Nor could there be any doubt that S.D.'s inability to set the post into the hole, symbolically, represented his inability to insert his penis into his wife's vagina. In the dream he had to give up the idea of 'erecting the fence', [S.D.'s words] undoubtedly symbolically referring to his own impotency because of his inability to have an erection.[61] [62] It is no coincidence that he was able to put up four posts, but not the fifth.—He was potent up to the fifth decade of his life.—What now follows emerged during his therapeutic sessions with me.

Becoming an entrepreneur was an attempt to change his status from employee to employer, something which he indicated was very important to him. As he put it, "To become 'numero uno'." Undoubtedly, there would not have been a traumatic impact if his enterprise had been successful. But because of his failure, he perceived himself as a beaten, penniless failure. Because this trauma was more than he could cope with, the ICR phenomenon occurred. In his regressed, irrational state, he believe that he was being *punished* for his *aggression*, for which he felt overwhelmingly guilty. Several times during his sessions with me, he proclaimed, "I am being punished for my greed...I should have left well enough alone," referring to his comfortable role as an employee. He told me that during his depression, he often discussed his greed with his wife who tried, without success, to dissuade him from his belief.

---

61 The tremendous popularity of the 'wonder' drug, Viagra, indicates the prevalence of sexual impotency.
62 Finch, Stewart and Cain, Albert; Psychoanalysis of Children; Basic Books; N.Y., 1968, p. 443.

His depression was so intense that he no longer could function, i.e., deal with the reality of his financial devastation. He never perceived his sexual impotency as punishment. The connection was made after he started treatment with me. It was only then that he perceived his wish to be 'numero uno', as a symbolic representation be the head of the family, i.e., to replace his father. The fantasy of replacing one's parent, to have total possession of the other parent, is a very common fantasy of the child. The latter is a common fantasy which often is extremely guilt producing. In adults it is the equivalent of taking on the role of God, the omnipotent and the omniscient.[63]—If his enterprise had succeeded, he never would have experienced the ICR. He might have grown in stature.

Summary: The case study dream dramatically illustrates the following four concepts:

1) The manifest and latent content of the dream.

The manifest content of the dream is the fence and all the related problems. The latent content is the aggression related to replacing his father, the guilt and the punishment, i.e. his banktuptcy and his impotence.—Although S.D. was impotent, he still retained a biological sexual drive, as manifested by his recurrent dream of trying to erect the fence.—This case is an excellent example of the AGP syndnrome.

2) Dream symbolism:

1 pole = penis;

2 hole, the receptacle for the post = vagina;

3 inability to place post in hole = impotency;

4 forgo the 'erection of the fence' = give up attempts at sex;

---

63 In the previous chapter I explained how sometimes you remember only a name, irrelevant words, a phrase, even a single word, a part of a melody or a bit of anything else. Whatever it is should be recorded.

5 fifth hole = fifth decade of life.

3) Dream analysis:

S.D.'s dream was a manifestation of his frustrated sexuality. In reality, he had no interest in sex at the time we met. But in his unconscious, the biological sexual drive was still active. It emerged in the form of recurrent dreams, which sybolically represented his unsuccessful attempts to find an outlet for his repressed sexuality.

4) The AGP syndrome:

The AGP syndrome is dramatically portrayed in S.D.'s recurrent dream. His aggression, guilt and punishment were all symolized in the manifest content of his dream. The ICR phenomenon, i.e., his inability to cope with his financial debacle and his sexual impotency, appeared in the manifest content of his dream. But because of the phenomena of regression and repression, he was able to continue to function on a reality level, ie. 'the show stayed on the road'.

CHAPTER 11

STEP I: The Dream: Part 2

The Moss Method for Self-Analysis consists of six steps:

I The Dream

II The List

III Directed Associations: (DA)

IV Non-Directed Associations: (NDA)

V Recapitulation

VI Analytic Interpretation (Search for Insight)

The practical procedures of each of the above steps will be dealt with in great detail. The first five steps are intended as preparation for carrying out the the sixth and final step, in which insight is achieved. The latter is done by correlating and analyzing the cumulated material of all of the five previous steps. In contrast to the last chapter that dealt only with the theoretical aspects of the dream, this chapter deals with the practical procedure of dealing with the dream.

Although many say that they never dream, the fact is that everyone dreams. Those who say they don't dream simply do not remember that they did. They have amnesia of their dream.

Three examples of such amnesia are: I) A person is awakened from deep sleep in the middle of the night by loud street noise such as the backfire of an automobile, fire engines with their loud sirens, etc. Some may even turn on the lights or look out of the window and then immediately fall back to sleep. Upon awakening the following morning, the person may have no recollection of having been awakened. 2) Upon awakening from deep sleep one often talks incoherently in a brief exchange of words with another person nearby, yet in the morning one has total amnesia of the incident. 3) Those who sleepwalk, or those who talk in their sleep, may remember nothing if not awakened. If reminded, some individuals might recall while others recall nothing.

Because dreams are often so fickle, some that you recall vividly when you wake up in the morning are forgotten during the brief moment it takes to record them in your notebook. But there are strategies that you can employ to assist in remembering your dreams. What follows are some practical hints for remembering dreams:

1. When awakened with a dream during the night, record it immediately into a tape recorder. This requires that you keep your tape recorder within arm's reach. Learn how to operate it in the dark so that it will not be necessary to turn on the lights. A voice operated recorder is ideal for this purpose

2. One of the reasons that you don't remember your dream is that you never made an effort to remember it. You assume you don't dream and that's the end of it. Once you change your attitude and realize that you dream but just don't remember it, then do the following: Suggest to yourself several times before falling asleep, "I shall awaken with a dream tonight. I shall remember my dream." It is usually necessary to repeat this autosuggestion several successive nights. Eventually, you will remember that

you had a dream, but that you forgot it. This is progress because now you know that you do dream just like everyone else does. Always continue with your autosuggestions as you lay your head on the pillow for sleep.

But one thing is certain, that is that once you you start to engage in systematic self-analysis you will remember your dreams. I have treated a number of individuals who started out as 'nondreamers'. All of them started to remember their dreams soon after treatment was started. It never fails. That is because the analytic process breaks down resistance. You must not allow yourself to become discouraged. That in itself is resistance

The practical procedure requires two things: 1) a small portable tape recorder that you will keep at your bedside. 2) a notebook and pen or pencil. I prefer a ball point pen. Starting with step one and with all the remaining steps, everything is to be entered into your notebook.

There are three stages of entering your dream into your note book. 1) At first, the dream is spoken into a tape recorded. 2) It is then transferred from the recorder into your notebook in brief outline form. 3) Later the dream is rewritten in detail. These three steps will now be explained.

1) The recorder should be small and must be within reach at your bedside—as indicated relative to remembering your dream.—When you awaken in the morning with a dream, you must imediately record the dream. But there are times during the night that you may awaken with a dream. It is optional whether you should record it or just go back to sleep. If it is easy for you to fall asleep again, then you should record it.—Do not record the minute details of a long dream if that will awaken you and you will not be able to fall asleep again.—However, if falling asleep again is a problem, it would be better to go back to sleep without recording your dream. You must decide which is the

lesser of the two evils, depriving yourself of sleep or losing the dream. If you are experiencing a period of acute emotional distress, it would be better to record the dream. If you can't fall asleep, then get up and proceed with a self-analytic session. A successful session is better than the best sleep aid medication.

2) Transfer the dream from the tape recorder to your notebook immediately after you get out of bed in the morning. This must be done before you do any of your morning routine. Some dreams are so fragile that although the details are vivid upon awakening, you may lose the entire dream instantaneously; sometimes, even as you are reaching for the recorder. You have it in your head in all its details, feeling confident you'll remember it, but it may be gone the next instant. This sometimes happens when you attend to other matters, toilette, eating, etc. This entry at this time should be brief and sketchy. It should not contain the details of the dream but rather only an overview of what the dream is about.[64] This is especially true if you have a long and complicated dream and/or if you have more than one dream. Once you write the brief highlights of your dream, you may then take care of the necessary toilette details. Sometimes upon awakening, you are certain that you dreamed but you can't remember a single fragment of it. Nevertheless, later in the day, on your way to your office, or even during a session with your patient, the dream may emerge with full vividness. Make a note of it to

---

64 If you think rationally, you will consider yourself just as important, or even more so, than your patient. Therefore, you should treat yourself accordingly. You will consider the appointment with yourself as the most important one of the day. If you do not perceive yourself in this light, you will always find excuses and rationalize reasons why you don't have the time. If this is the case, you must be honest with yourself and recognize your resistance to change, which is no different than the resistance of your patients.

deal with it in your next session. I often rearrange my schedule to do this because I perceive this kind of recall as a window of opportunity about something important going on in my life.

3) After your usual wake-up morning routine, you return to your desk/table to elaborate on the details of your dream, which up to now was only a brief listing. It is better to do this even before breakfast while the dream is still fresh in your memory. Delay, for whatever reason, often results in memory loss of some part of your dream, especially the emotional aspect of the dream. The sooner you elaborate on the dream, the more is the likelihood that you will retain the full emotional impact.

At this point I digress to repeat the admonition I gave you in the first chapter, "Mind Set:" the most important goal in your life should be to strive for continued emotional growth, maturation, well-being and happiness. If this is your goal, you will make necessary changes in your daily schedule. This includes rising early enough in the morning to have a self-analysis session. You might say, "But this means getting up five o'clock in the morning."[65]

To this I answer, "That is not necessary, if you make your first appointment of the day with yourself." Or you can make the appointment with yourself later in the day, such as before or after your lunch break. But it is preferable before you see your first patient. As mentioned above, much of the dream material is lost with the passage of time when the exigencies of the day crowd the dream out of your mind.

"But that will cut down the number of appointments with my patients. It will cut into my income."

"What is more important, your income or your well being and happiness?" I ask. If you are hesitant about the answer, I suggest

---

65 Jacobs, Theodore, MD; Seminar of The Soc. of the NY School for Psychotherapists. March 8, 1998.

that you to reread and ponder over the footnote. It's easy to be convinced intellectually of the correct answer, but that is not enough. You must get the gut feeling that you are more important than anything else in your life. With this feeling you will find the time for your appointment with yourself.

Although the above dialogue was a diversion, I deemed it necessary to put it into the text. The tremendous resistance against confrontation of the unconscious is no less for you than it is for your patients. I agree with Dr. Jacobs who says, "...You must confront your own demons to exorcise them out of your unconscious."[66] To do this, you must make a commitment to yourself to make growth and emotional maturation the most important goal of your life. If you carry out that commitment, you will make available the time you need for your fifty-minute (or longer) daily sessions with yourself.

With this digression I now discuss the time to be spent on this Step I, The Dream. There is great variation in the time necessary for this step, depending on the length and elaboration of the dream details. It may vary from less than two minutes to as much as fifteen minutes. There is a detailed breakdown of the time for each step in the epilogue

The next chapter deals with Step 11, The List.

---

66 If there were no other reason to learn and practice self analysis, this alone would be sufficient, even though I believe it is not the major reason. The latter should be to improve the quality of your life.

CHAPTER 12

STEP II: THE LIST

After the dream has been entered into your notebook, with all the detailed elaboration, you proceed with Step 11, The List. This consists of entering into your notebook a list of all currently disturbing problems, emotions, etc. When discussing the unconscious mind, I stressed the fact that it is active and functioning at all times, awake or asleep, from the start of life until death. At any given moment, some part of the unconscious is activated by what is ongoing in one's overt reality at that moment, the HERE and NOW.(H&N). The H&N activates any and all associations that emerge into consciousness. The reverse is also true. For every conscious emotion there is a concomitant unconscious reaction. Think of a stone thrown into a calm body of water, like a lake. The rippling waves one sees are similar to the waves created in the unconscious mind, but with one difference; the water waves are only horizontal, whereas, in the unconscious the waves also travel 'vertically' and even 'diagonally' through different strata of the past, (i.e., infancy, early and late childhood, puberty, adolescence etc.)

In Chapter 2, I discussed in great detail how everything of the past is stored forever in one's unconscious mind, just like input stored in the memory of a computer. Since the H&N activates a response on all levels of the unconscious, analysis probes and investigates these various levels of response. Everything that emerges during the analytic session in either dyadic or self-analysis, including the dream, results from ongoing reality of one's life, i.e., the H&N. Within the framework of that reality are three categories of activities:

1) Those that are done routinely. They generally have a negligible emotional involvement in the unconscious. Examples include getting dressed to go to work, eating, shopping, participating in sports, entertainment, etc.

2) Events, activities or preoccupations that result in some degree of emotional change ranging from a mild case of over-reaction and/or irrational thinking, irrational behavior to a state of acute emotional distress that sometimes involves neurotic and/or psychosomatic symptoms. Examples include altercations with employer/employee, spouse, or child, a serious accident resulting in injury to yourself or to others, significant financial setback, loss of a loved one, past or performance anxiety about an upcoming sexual encounter, and hundreds of other events of a disturbing nature. Any of the foregoing would be an item on your list. A disturbing incident with your patient during an analytic session resulting in countertransference (CTR) should also be on your list.[67]

---

67 As a practicing dentist for many years, I have encountered scores of people with such phobias. It may seem incredible that one was a psychoanalyst whom I had to hypnotize to be able to do his dental work.

3) A state of emotional elation. Examples of emotional elation include: winning a sweepstakes; sudden fame in sports or theater; birth of a child; graduating from school; passing the bar or state exam to be licensed to practice your profession.

What is an intense emotional response for one person might be relatively free of emotional response for another. For example an appointment with the dentist for one individual has practically no emotional response, while for another it may be tremendous, especially one with a dental phobia. He/she may fret for days prior to his/her dental appointment.[68]

With the above explanation, I now proceed to discuss Step 11. After your dream has been entered into your notebook with all the detailed elaboration, you proceed to Step 11, The List. You should list of all activities, events, actions or thoughts that are ongoing in your life that produce an emotional response, i.e., anxiety, frustration, guilt, fear, etc. All associations that emerge during the analytic session originate from the list, or in some way are related to the list. The list is like an umbrella that covers all associations and material that will later emerge as the analytic session evolves. The umbrella also includes the dream since the dream is a spin-off of one or more items on the list originating in the H&N.

The actual procedure of Step 11 starts with listing all disturbing problems, emotions, preoccupations, anxieties, etc. with which you are currently concerned. These items comprise the material to be dealt with and analyzed later in the session. The items must be numbered in the order in which they come to your mind.

---

68 You can not control what's in your unconscious. The most you can do is to confront it and deal with it. To do the latter usually cancels out its impact on your perception and behavior.

The number of items that comprise the list varies from three or four to as many as eight to ten, depending on what preoccupies your thoughts and emotions regarding the H&N. For me it is usually about five to seven items. But there are days that it is as high as ten or more. The dream is always item #1 on the list. Even if you have no dream, it is still item #1, but listed as, 'no dream'. It is assumed that every item on the list derives from something ongoing in your life, your H&N. It is also assumed that every ongoing emotion, intense enough to be on the list, has an unconscious concomitant, perhaps a dream or a traumatic memory that you probably repressed. Very often, as your session progresses, you remember your dream. This is because enough resistance has been removed during the session to allow the dream to emerge. For this reason, the 'no dream' entry is a significant item on the list.

The items on the list should be no more than one or two words. The word is the label that represents the item. That is sufficient because you have all the detailed information about the item in your head. A single word is a cue for the entire item. In this way you don't loose time so that you can move right on to the next step.

What follows are two sample lists. The first, List #1, my own hypothetical list:

List #1
1) dream
2) writing (this book)
3) Joan
4) eat
5) sex
6) Ethel

What follows is the explanation of each of the foregoing items. Although each item actually appeared on my list at different times during the past months, I bunched them together to make them all appear on the same day. I did this in order to show the relation, i.e., connection, between all of the items. Later in this chapter I shall discuss the significance of the connection.

1) Dream. I am not describing the details of the dream because the use of a cue word refers to the detailed notebook entry of the dream.

2) Writing. This book has been quite a challenge to me. It created fantasies that have very deep roots in my life. Although I do not consciously perceive myself as a superior individual, my unconscious perceives writing this book as a highly aggressive act, i.e., I am taking on the role of my father.[69] This activates Oedipal fantasies.[70]

3) Joan. The name of a very wealthy woman who is my friend. She is seventy-five years old. Recently she made a new will in which I was appointed executor and major beneficiary. If I outlive her I stand to inherit more than a million dollars. But there is a problem. Since she made the will, she has become manipulative, quarrelsome, belligerent and demanding. I am losing my patience at her increasing provocations. It's getting beyond my tolerance so that I'm tempted to wash my hands of her. With that amount of money involved, I am in conflict about the situation. All the foregoing is represented by the word, Joan.

4) Eat. Last night when I went out to dinner with friends, I ate and drank too much. My lack of control resulted in self-abuse.

5) Sex. Last night I was a failure at my attempt at sex. I was impotent. This has become a rare occurrence for me.

---

69 Elaboration of the preceding material is irrelevant at this time, since our attention is focused on The List. I shall return to this material later on in this chapter.

70 For a detailed description of this case refer to Chapters 8 and 9.

6) Ethel. Ethel is a pseudonym for my sister, three-and-a-half years younger than me. We exchanged angry words yesterday. Our relationship is at a low point. Ethel, is frequently on my list.

The second list, unlike the first, is a list actually taken from the case of MB, the CEO who discharged an employee, case discussed in chapters 8. What follows are the cue words on MB's list.

List #2

1 dream

2 argument

3 keys

4 eat

A brief review of what MB told me now follows.:[71] "Yesterday I had a distressing altercation with a subordinate, female worker. I decided to discharge her, a decision about which I felt very guilty. Upon leaving my office and arriving at the garage where my car was parked, I could not find my car keys. I searched my brief case and my large shoulder bag. It was in vain. They had to break into my car. This was a mess that intensified my already greatly distress state. Before going to bed that night, I went on a binge and raided the refrigerator. With the discomfort of a stuffed stomach, I tossed and turned for hours before I fell asleep." After a brief pause she continued. "I had a frightening dream. I was being chased by a woman. I ran and ran but could not escape from her pursuit. There was much more, but I can't remember what it was."

The cue words are practically self-explanatory. The word ARGUMENT represented the altercation with her employee; KEY, the problems that ensued and EAT, the out-of-control binge before going to bed. The case of MB will again be discussed in the last chapter, "Analytic Interpretation."

---

71 Berryman, John; 1914-72; Pulitzer prize winning poem, *His Rest*; 1968.

There are times when an item should be on your list because of a current problem or disturbance. You repressed the memory of that item even though it may have been the most significant item on the list. But you forgot about it. Later in your session, you suddenly remember that item. Whenever this happens, as it will occasionally, you must immediately stop what you are doing and go back and add it to the list. It was something you repressed but were able to recover as the analytic session evolved. The recollection of that item may be a key that opens doors to important associations .

There may be an item on your list that is carried over from the previous day. This item may be on your list for several successive days or even weeks. Examples of such items include a problem with your child or spouse, financial difficulties, bodily injury resulting from an accident, or an alarming result of a biopsy. These are just a few that might be carried over from a previous session.

Occasionally an item recurs for a period of days or weeks then may not appear again for months or longer. The problem may have been temporarily resolved and disappears and only occurs again weeks, months or years later. For example, if you had a cancer free biopsy report, but you were told that you must return in six months for another checkup. You will have the same anxiety you had only six months later. It will be on your list for the second time around. Another example is a resolved conflict with your spouse. The problem emerged again at a later date. Domestic altercations are an example of such a problem. Childhood sexual assault or rape are examples of traumas that will periodically be on your list if something in your ongoing reality activates the past.

Another reason for a recurring item on your list is that it may be a problem that you have dealt with in the past, but at the time you could advance no further with that problem. Then as you progress with your self-analysis, e.g., weeks, months or even years later, you will have grown and matured and have a stronger ego, all of which lowers your resistance. You will come back again and deal with the past on a deeper level than previously. John Berryman, an American poet laureate who died in 1972 expressed the concept of the recurrent past as follows: "...and it seems that the search continues until we die. We reach out after each new beginning, penetrating our context to know ourselves; and our knowledge increases until we recognize again, more profoundly each time, our pain, indignity and triviality. This is the bitter cup that is offered; heaped with curses..."[72]

The same concept is also expressed by T.S. Eliot in his famous poem, *The Wasteland:*

> We shall not cease from exploration
> And the end of all our exploring
> Will be to arrive where we started
> And know the place for the first time...[73]

A childhood trauma remains in your unconscious forever. Nothing is ever forgotten by the unconscious! The trauma will recur in your dreams throughout your life. With self-analytic progress, you may often dream about it, but each time you return to the repressed trauma, its impact on your life is diminished. At age ninety, a sexual trauma that I suffered at age ten still continues to emerge in my dreams, in symbolic form, of course. But now, its impact on my life is minimal. There are recurrences of other incidents in my past such as sibling rivalry, guilt for all my unfaithful behavior and finally the dissolution of my marriage, which my unconscious perceives as deserting my

---

72 Eliot, T(homas) S(teans), 1888-1965; *The Wasteland*, 1922.
73 See Chapter 8, Fantasy Constellation.

own child.[74] By my self-analysis *"I know the place for the first time."* [T.S.Eliot] I believe that my older colleagues whose life style include systematic self-analysis will be more attuned to the insights of these poets, (John Berryman and T.S.Eliot) than my younger colleagues.

I am resigned to the fact that my past will never will be eliminated from my unconscious; that I'll have to deal with ALL OF MYSELF for the rest of my life. What part of my past emerges in my dreams is determined by the H&N items on my list in Step 11. Thus, the items on the list in Step 11 deal with the past as they do with the present. Dealing with the present will lead you to your past. Each time you discover your past through the analytic process, you will understand yourself much better; you will be more in control of your life.

The time for Step 11 should not take more than five minutes. When the list is completed, you immediately move on to Steps 111, ?Free Association,? the title of the next chapter.

---

74 There are two kinds of FREE ASSOCIATION(FA) as it applies to the Moss Method. This is a concept different from the generally accepted meaning. When you direct your attention to a given thought or object, the associations that emerge are known as DIRECTED ASSOCIATIONS (DAs). When you allow your mind to be passive with no attention given to anything, the associations that emerge are called NON DIRECTED ASSOCIATIONS (NDAs). In this chapter and for the rest of this book, three abbreviations will be used: 1) FA for free association, 2) DA for directed association and 3) NDA for nondirected association

CHAPTER 13⁷⁵

STEPS III and IV: FREE ASSOCIATION

STEP 111: DA: This chapter deals with the practical aspects of Step 111 and Step 1V. After compiling the list in Step 11, there should be no delay, if possible, in pursuing the remaining steps of the Moss Method. But if you must postpone your session for later in the day, you should start from scratch and make a new list. New events may have taken place in the interim, which might alter the original list that you made earlier in the day.

With The Dream and the list already entered into your notebook, you direct your attention to both your dream and your list. Your unconcious will determing which of the two takes presidence. Whatever associations or thoughts that come to your mind are entered into your notebook. This will be critically examined and analyzed in the last step of The Moss Method.

Free Association (FA) is a phenomenon that we all experience, although most of the time we are not aware that it is occurring. There are always a myriad of extraneous thoughts, ideas, feelings,

---

75 This is the first time the concept of THOUGHT PROVOKER appears in the professional literature.

experiences and emotions popping in and out of our mind. Your mind is constantly being bombarded by stimuli. We then find a conscious reason for our behavaior; we rationalize our uneasiness, fear and/or anxiety without knowing that the reason lies in the unconscious. In chapter six, I discussed the phenomenon of rationalization when I described the posthypnotic suggestion given to the subject to open the window. The need to open the window came from the subject's unconscious and not from his rationalizations.

An example of such bombardment of the senses often occurs when we meet an individual the first time. Without realizing it, we note the color of eyes, wrinkles on skin, mole, beauty mark, disheveled clothing, soiled shirt, quality of voice, physical stature, body odor, teeth, resemblance to aunt, teacher, friend, foe, etc. FAs are occurring continuously throughout the day, regardless of anything you may be doing or what may be happening. You may be driving a car, reading a book, washing dishes, shaving, dressing, combing your hair, preparing meals, shopping, playing tennis, swimming, studying, walking the streets, riding the bus or subway, before, during, and/or after sexual activity , on a plane, —especially while strapped to your seat during takeoff—etc. The list of stimuli and situations is innumerable. As a therapist, the bombardment of stimuli coming from your patient while on the couch during treatmant, is of paramount importance. Your systematic daily self-analysis will put you in charge of your contertransference instead of your uncontrolable unconscious.

Whatever emerges into consciousness is not an accident or coincidence. No thought or association is haphazard, arising out of nowhere. Every thought is PROVOKED by something originating either from the internal environment, i.e., from within your own mind, or from the external environment, your physical self or your surroundings. There is a reason why any thought reaches consciousness, though that reason may not be known or apparent. We are often unaware of the provocation. The concept of provocation is a very important factor in free association. The Moss Method leans heavily on this concept. In Step III you intentionally direct your attention to your dream and/or your list in order to provoke FAs. Thus, whatever thoughts or associations emerge in Step III are not an accident or coincidence. They are associations that you provoked. Free associations may be a single thought or may be complicated as in a reverie or a day dream of "castles in the sky." The thought may be one of a fleeting nature or one that is sustained over a period of several minutes.

The Moss Method distinguishes between two kinds of free association.[76] The first I named, DIRECTED ASSOCIATION (DA), because in Step III, your attention is directed to your dream and/or your list. In contrast, in step IV you try think of nothing attempting to make your mind go blank. You are 'free wheeling.' You do not direct your attention to anything. The associations that emerge are NONDIRECTED ASSOCIATION (NDA).

If there is a delay or postponement of resuming your session from the time when the dream was entered into your notebook, try to remember the dream without rereading your notes. If you can't remember the dream, or any part of the dream, then reread the dream as it was written and add it to your notes before proceeding with Step III (Naturally if there was no dream to record this cannot be done.)The reason for trying to remember the dream is to compare what is now recalled with what was originally written down. If there is a difference, such as something written down originally but now left out because it was forgotten, it must be dealt with as RESISTANCE for that item. The same reason is the same as that when dealing with 'forgetting'

---

76 See Chapter 2, "The Concealed World of the Unconscious."

items when making the list in Step II. Recalling forgotten parts of your dream provokes important associations. In summary, Step 111. and Step IV are designed to gather material to enter into your notebook. What now follows is the procedure for Step 111.

Step 111: DA You start by sitting comfortably at your desk or writing table, with notebook and pencil in hand. Direct your attention to your dream and your list. Write anything that comes to your mind. You are not to screen out or censor any DAs even if you think they are trivial, irrelevant or unimportant. To deal with a DA in this manner, is a form of resistance that I call NEGATIVE TRIVIALIZATION, a phenomenon which will be dealt with in the final step of the Moss Method.

Sometimes your DAs may come in such rapid succession as to be almost simultaneous. It is often impossible to write fast enough to record them all. For this reason you must develop a form of speed writing which I call ANALYTIC WRITING. Your normal writing-speed would tend to hold back, and perhaps lose, some DA's that emerge. Your analytic writing must keep pace with your thoughts. A moment's delay is enough of a time lapse to lose important DAs. Abbreviate as much as possible. You need not include word endings, such as, 'ing' and/or 'tion'. Words should appear almost as cues or graphic representations. After all, no one but you will read these notes. Once the words are down on paper, regardless of how badly written, you will almost always recognize the word picture, since it is the thought behind the collection of words that is important. You will discover that the writing jumps right up to conscious recognition. Correct spelling is irrelevant. One of my former patients, a psychoanalyst, told me that he can type almost as fast as he can think. Do the same if you can.

I have found that the use of a tape recorder for the above to be impractical. The reason is that later on in steps V, and VI you must scan your notes very rapidly and allow your unconscious to SELECT certain portions of your written notes. This can not be done effectively with a tape recorder.—The phenomenon of SELECTIVITY will be discussed in detail in the last step of the Moss Method—.

In Step 111 you are not to attempt to analyze or to make any sense about what you write. Nor should you spend time rereading anything. This will be done in Step V, the next chapter, "Recapitulation." Keep writing whatever DAs emerge. You continue gathering DAs for about ten minutes. It's optional to spend more time. This depends on how much time you've allowed for the session. The time for each of the six steps will be discussed later on in the book. Now, you may proceed with Step IV, collecting NDAs.

STEP IV: NDA. In the previous step, Step 111, your intellect was involved. You voluntarily directed your attention at your written notes and recorded whatever DAs emerged into your consciousness. In contrast, Step IV necessitates a learning process. The method of gathering of material must be totally devoid of your intellect. This step is done by 'free wheeling', i.e., going wherever your unconscious takes you without interference from your will or intellect. You must strive for total detachment, total passivity; you must 'let go' and try to relax as though going to sleep. But you must not allow yourself to fall asleep. The tendency sometimes may exist. Falling asleep is a cop-out, which is a manifestation of resistance. Obviously, while asleep, the entire analytic process ceases. The process necessitates a new kind of discipline that must be learned. At first it might seem impossible to do, but I assure you that you can learn the procedure.

DAs often emerge in the form of fantasies flitting in and out of consciousness, often leaving no trace in the conscious mind. It is those whimsical, capricious thoughts that Step IV endeavors to capture. You must learn to catch the thoughts or fantasies 'by the tail' as they rapidly recede into oblivion. You must endeavor to retrieve the CHAIN OF THOUGHT or any links or bits of that chain that crop up and immediately disappear.

Everything that crops up into your mind in Step IV has a direct or indirect bearing on one or more items listed in Step 11. These items and the dream originate from the H&N. These captured DAs and NDAs are not the actual unconscious emotions for which one searches, but rather a *symbolic* representation. They are analogous to the manifest content of a dream. The decoding or deciphering of these symbolic representations is done in Step VI.

To many readers, the phenomenon of NDA will be an entirely new experience, an unfamiliar mental activity. After describing what this entails, I then shall give specific, detailed instructions for how this step is done. This chapter will end with an experiment in free association. It is intended for all readers, especially those who have never practiced or experienced the phenomenon of free association. A method of self scoring will be given to determine the degree of success achieved in carrying out this experiment.

In dyadic analysis, during periods of silence, you keep prompting your patient with the questions, "What are you thinking of?...What's on your mind?" Need I remind you, the analyst, that the patient very often says, "Nothing, my mind was blank." But you know that it is not so. The analyst teaches the patient to capture those fleeting thoughts. In self-analysis, you are both the patient who produces NDAs and the therapist who captures and records them. Totally contradictory patterns of mental activity must occur. You are attempting to achieve a state of total passivity. Then while in this detached state, you must suddenly arouse yourself into a state of intellectual alertness in order to hold on to or retrieve what is about to slip back into the oblivion. I use the metaphor "Catch the thought by the tail", for retrieving fleeting thoughts.

Since Step IV requires that you learn the discipline of assuming the role of both the patient and the therapist, there are those who say it can't be done. My answer to them is that I've been doing self-analysis successfully for about fifty years. I've also taught many others the procedure. A prosthesis, e.g., a denture or an artificial leg, is not the same as one's own anatomy, but it enables a person to eat or to walk. However, I agree that the help of a therapist is more efficient in the same way that your own anatomy is better than a prosthesis.The same holds true in regard to being your own therapist.

What now follows is a 15 minute exercise. It is intended for those who have never had analytic experience, i,e,. those who are not even cognizant of the phenomenon. If your training-analysis was a success, you have already experienced the phenomenon of NDA. Therefore, the following experiment is optional for those of you who don't need the instruction. *Before proceeding with the experiment*, you should first read and understand the instructions that follow.

START OF EXPERIMENT

INSTRUCTIONS: Find an isolated place where there is minimal distraction or interference from noises, telephones, doorbells, people, etc. It is best to assume a reclining posture. Have a notebook and a pencil within reach. Close your eyes. This will help to eliminate outside stimulation or distraction so that all associations are provoked from within. Think of nothing. Let the mind go blank. Relax both mind and body. Try to forget that you are performing an experiment. Bring all intellectual activity to a halt. Ask yourself no questions. Do not try to understand the purpose of this experiment. Be as passive as possible. Keep eyes closed all time. Take several very deep breaths to relax your diaphram. Think of nothing, Let your mind go blank...blank... blank Let yourself drift into a state of reverie. It may require from one to five minutes to achieve this state. Be patient. It's a new experience. At any time that you become aware of a thought or a series of thoughts, pull yourself out of the reverie; get up instantly and write the results in your notebook. If while writing, new thoughts emerge, write them also. Once your thoughts are written down, proceed as before. Lie down; make yourself comfortable; again take several deep breaths; try again to become passive. Let your mind go blank...blank...blank...Wait until a thought or thoughts emerge as happened the previous time. Add the information to your notes. Repeat this several more times over a period of about 10 minutes.

STOP READING: Proceed with the experiment.

By what criteria can you judge this experiment as a success or failure? There are three possibilities: 1) success, 2) partial success and 3) failure.

Success The ability to capture and to recall any part of your train of thoughts that are entered into your notebook. You may have as many as a half dozen NDAs flitting in and out of your mind. Often, the most you can retrieve is only a small fraction of them. That is sufficient to claim success.

Partial success You know that there were thoughts flitting in and out of your mind, but you were unable to retrieve any. This is considered a partial success since you are cognizant of having had thoughts, even though you couldn't retrieve any. This is in contrast to failure.

Failure No awareness of having had any thoughts. The mind was blank throughout the entire period.

This experiment must be repeated as often as necessary until you score a success. With some it may happen the firsl time.

Others may have to do this experiment several times to score a success. Sometimes it is necessary to repeat the experiment at a future time in order to achieve success. It is futile to attempt Step Vl, the final step of the Moss Method, until you can achieve success in this experiment. Once success is obtained you may proceed to the next chapter, Step V: "Recapitulation".

CHAPTER 14

STEP V: RECAPITULATION

The purpose of Step V is to continue to gather additional raw material in preparation for Step VI, the final step. Then the material will be processed and analyzed.

In the previous chapter I discussed the phenomenon of PROVOCATION in order to produce DAs. I indicated that whatever thought crops up into consciousness is not an accident. There is always a stimulus, either from the internal environment or from the external environment that PROVOKES whatever thoughts or associations. It's a cause and effect relationship; the cause is the provocation (stimulus); the effect is one or more associations. Based on this cause and effect phenomenon, I devised a series of four THOUGHT PROVOKERS (TPs)which are utilized in the Moss Method.[77]

The following are the four TPs:

---

77 In Chapter 6, "We Are All Hypnotic Subjects," I explained that the subject opened the window because of a posthypnotic suggestion planted in his unconscious. He was unaware that his need to open the window was motivated by his unconscious.

1 Reviewing Your Notes (all or part)

2 Recall (past experiences)

3 Questions Directed to Yourself

4 Critical Scrutinization

Although what follows is a discussion of all four TPs, the first, reviewing your notes, is the only one of the four that is used in Step V. The remaining three TPs are applied in the final step, analysis and interpretation. Like in the previous steps, whatever new associations emerge from this step are generally in symbolic form. The process of decoding of the symbolism is dealt with in the final step of the Moss Method. After a brief overview of the four TPs, I shall describe the procedure for Step V.

1) REVIEWING NOTES: It is presumed that by the time you arrive at Step V, you have accumulated from one to three pages of notes. The rationale of going back and reading your notes is as follows: By reading your notes, you are bombarding your unconscious with the accumulated material gathered up to now. This starts a flow of new associations because of some degree of lowered resistance, compared to what you had at the start of Step 111. With the lowered resistance, new associations are more directly related to the repressed material in the unconscious than were the original associations.

2) RECALL EMOTIONALLY TRAUMATIC EXPERIENCES: For this your intellect again is voluntarily involved. You must make a concerted effort to recall the experiences that left their indelible effects on your psyche, even though you never before done so willfully.— In chapter two I discussed the case of the forty-five year old physician who under hypnosis relived the bloody trauma that happened when he was three-and-a-half years old. Likewise, every traumatic experience you ever had is permanently carved into your psyche.—The process of recalling serves as a powerful

TP that releases a train of associations.. Like in the previous steps these new DAs must be added to your notes.

3) QUESTIONS to yourself: The idea of talking to yourself may seem ridiculous; but the character of the unconscious is also ridiculous?[78] The questions to yourself are TPs that provoke DAs (directed associations) the same way as when you directed your attention to your dream and your list in Step 111, Chapter 12. This TP will be amply discussed when dealing with the final step of the Moss Method.

4) CRITICAL SCRUTINIZATION: This is the most significant TP. It consists of reviewing and working with everything that you have recorded in your notebook up to now. By the time you get to this stage of your analytic session, the constant bombardment of the unconscious will have significantly lowered your resistance to the degree that make interpretation and insight possible. The foregoing was a very brief discussion of the four TPs used with the Moss Method. What now follows is the procedure for Step V.

You are seated at your desk with your notes in front of you. Starting with your dream, you rapidly scan your notes, allowing your eyes to selectively stop where they will. At this time, you still do not read your notes. It may seem incredible that although you believe that you control what you select, the fact is that it is your unconscious that determines what you focus on and read.[79] With the resistance lowered, part of your notes selected by your unconscious will literally jump up at you. This causes more associations to crop up. Stop reading and immediately add to

---

78 See chapter 8, "Fantasy Constellation."

79 When anxiety is irrationally exaggerated, I have found it to be an important clue of an unconscious wish. The significance of this will be dealt with in the next chapter.

your notes whatever new thoughts come to your mind. You are still in the process of gathering raw material. Do not censor any thought that crops up. The same rule about negative trivialization applies in this step as it does in the previous steps. Nothing that emerges should be trivialized. Every thought must be entered into your notes.

After entering the new associations, go back to where you left off the scanning process and continue to the end, always adding to your notes as before. When you come to the end of your written material, go back to the beginning, repeating the scan/write process. Allow yourself about ten minutes for this step.

There are two subjects covered in this chapter:

1) Utilization of the first TP, i.e., scanning your notes: Whatever emerges is directly or indirectly related to your dream or to the items on your step 11 List—or should be on your list, but are forgotten (repressed).

2 The procedure of scan-couch-write, then back to your desk. It is a procedure that you must learn. In this step, as in the previous steps, there is still no attempt to be rational or to analyze any part of your notes.

CHAPTER 15

STEP VI: ANALYTIC INTERPRETATION
(Part One)

Step VI is presented in two parts, each occupying a chapter. This chapter, part one, deals with the fundamental concepts that form the basis for the practical procedures in the final step of the Moss Method. The next chapter, part two, deals with the practical procedure how to process the accumulated raw material in order to gain insight regarding the items on your list in Step 11, e.g., the H&N.

All your notes are the raw material, in symbolic language, related to one or more items on your list. It is analogous to the manifest content of your dream. Like with the dream, the latent contents can be achieved only by means of decoding (interpretation) of the written material. The strategy by which this is done involves knowing what to look for and knowing how to do it. Earlier in the book I referred to this as The What and The How. Applying the 'What-and-How' strategy results in a quantum leap forward in the success of self-analysis. In this chapter I shall discuss The WHAT. In the next and final chapter, I shall discuss the nitty-gritty details of The HOW.

In Section One of this book I discussed a number of concepts and/or phenomena, all of which form the foundation upon which the Moss Method is based. They are the following:

1. The unconscious continuously impacts on our conscious mind, often determining our perception and our behavior, yet we are oblivious of the phenomenon.
2. Every conscious emotion has a concomitant counterpart in the unconscious.
3. Emotions that are impossible to cope with are repressed and stored in the unconscious.
4. Resistance is one's defense against feeling (confronting) repressed material.
5. The unconscious is irrational, unable to distinguish between past, present and future; able to substitute and replace one person for another, or one person for a group of people, and visa versa; to displace your own emotions onto another person, or vice versa; to substitute a part of a person, place or event for the whole, or visa versa; to split one individual into several others all existing at the same time, e.g., your parent and yourself, your brother/sister and yourself;[80] to make a mountain out of a molehill or visa versa.
6. Whatever emerges into consciousness from the unconscious is usually in symbolic form that is usually unrecognizable to the conscious mind.
7. All past events, experiences, and emotions that ever occurred or existed in your life are permanently embedded in your unconscious. The original emotions connected to the trauma

---

80 An unconscious death wish is a common form of self punishment for the hostility and guilt toward parent resulting from parental discipline. Whatever hostility existed in childhood remains with you for your entire life.

may become activated and become the source of energy for the H&N ongoing emotional distress.

8. Neurotic symptoms—irrational thinking or compulsive behavior, psychosomatic etc.—are often the result of repression. The repressed material is converted into a symptom(s).

9. Every adult has a homeostatic balance between aggression, guilt and punishment, known as the AGP syndrome.

10. The unconscious usually reacts irrationally to traumatic events or experiences as though they were punishment for guilt.

11. No one is free of guilt. It starts to develop in infancy.

12 Repressed emotions have a noxious impact on our perception and behavior.

13 . Analytic insight of repressed emotions tends to cancel out the noxious impact on an individual's perception and behavior.

The chart that follows is a schematic illustration of the application of the the above list of premises. It is an oversimplification meant to be only schematic. On the left side are events and situations representing H&N, e.g., conscious emotons. On the right side are unconscious counterparts. The chart is a small sampling of possible entries sufficient to make the point that every conscious emotion has a counterpart in the unconscious. It goes without saying that everyone does not react in exactly the same way as indicated on the chart.—Note that the first three deal with the AGP syndrome. I'll explain the significance of this later in the text—.

CONSCIOUS	UNCONSCIOUS
1. Aggression (especially sexual)	Guilt, punishment
2 Guilt	Aggression, punishment
3. Mishap (traumatic)	Guilt, punishment

4. Irrational and intensified anxiety	Unconscious wish[81]
5. Confrontation with authority	Hostility, fear, guilt
6. Terminal illness of parent	Guilt, death wish for parent[82]
7. Marriage	Euphoria, aggression, guilt (Oedipal)
8. Criminal behavior	Aggression, guilt, punishment
9. Birth of first child	Euphoria, inadequacy (as parent)
10 Sex act	Euphoria, Aggression, Guilt, inadequacy

What now follows is a different list of premises that apply only to the Moss Method:

1 Although the unconscious seems to be chaotic, the Moss Method presumes that there is order to the nature and character of the unconscious.

2 All your written notes are related to one or more items on your list in Step 11.

3 All thoughts that crop up into consciousness (fleeting and instantly disappearing or retained for minutes or longer) are not an accident or coincidence. They are stimulated (provoked) by a stimulus originating either externally from environmental events, or internally from a previous thought. The latter is the rationale for the device I call "Thought Provokers" (TPs).

4 A series of continuous associations comprise a CHAIN in which each association is a LINK.

---

81 Since the name for this concept is my own creation, it will not be found in the literature.

82 Freud, S.; *New Introductory Lectures on Psychoanalysis*; Standard Edition; Hogarth Press, London, (Vol. 19, 1025) p. 173.

5 A reality with which one cannot cope results in an ICR (Impossible to Cope with Reality) phenomenon. This is an involuntary phenomenon that enables the individual to continue to function. The latter enables the individual to "keep the show on the road."

6 The Puddle-Of-Water (POW) logic: This utilizes the phenomenon of inductive reasoning which the dictionary defines as "the process of arriving at a general conclusion from observation of particular facts." The following is an example of POW logic:- If you look out of your window when you wake up in the morning and you see a puddle of water in your back-yard, you are sure that there was a downpour during the night. (The assumption is that the puddle of water could not have gotten there any other way.) Conversely, if you wake up in the middle of the night and you see a heavy downpour of rain, you are sure to find a puddle of water in your backyard when you wake up in the morning. The POW logic is a powerful tool when dealing with the AGP syndrome.

7 The final premise is that the Moss Method is feasible and can be learned. Its success depends on the degree to which you carry out the commitment to yourself to make emotional growth and maturity the most important goal of your life.

Since this chapter is directed to WHAT to look for in self-analysis, I start with the dream. What follows is a list of things that you can expect to find concealed in your dream. The order of the listing has no bearing on its relative importance or significance. Knowing what to look for is a giant step toward decoding the symbolism. Each item is disguised in symbolism:

1 resistance
2 denigration of the analytic process
3 the AGP syndrome
4 forgotten memories

5 sexuality

6 one or more items in Step 11, the List

I shall now discuss each item.

1) *Resistance* Emotions, conflicts and traumatic experiences that are too overwhelming to cope with (ICR) are repressed and lodged in the unconscious. Thus, there is resistance to cognizance of such material. Most dreams contain resistance, but it is concealed in symbolism.

2) *Denigration of the analytic process*: This is a manifestation of resistance. Discouragement, pessimism and futility are the arch enemies of analytic progress. Your thoughts may be, "Why should I waste my time and energy pursuing a procedure that has no validity and that doesn't work? Dr. Smith wrote a paper on the impossibility of being your own analyst because of the lack of objectivity? I'm working on this damn self-analysis for almost an hour, (a week, a month, etc.) and I'm getting nowhere."

3) *The AGP Syndrome*: This is one of the major cornerstones of The Moss Method. It exists in the unconscious of all of us. Since this already was discussed at great length, I shall postpone further discussion until the next chapter when I deal with the nitty-gritty details of the applications of the AGP syndrome to the analytic process.

4) *Forgotten Memories*: Past experiences or events keep recurring in our dreams. They may go as far back as infancy. Recall my description of the forty-five year old physician who at age three-and-a-half was traumatize by an accident in the playground. Since it was so traumatic, there is no doubt that the incident reoccurred frequently in his dreams; but he could never recognize it because it would appear in symbolic form. He might dream of only a part of that incident, such as a playground, a hospital, any kind of injury or accident to himself or to another person.

5) *Sexuality*: I find that almost always there is some element of my sexuality in my dreams. I am not referring to the obvious, e.g., when you wake up sexually aroused, but rather to the sexuality that is disguised in symbolism, unrecognizable until the dream is analyzed.

All of the information in this chapter should be at the fingertips of your mind. Like when driving a car, you keep looking at your side or back mirror before making a turn, passing another car on the highway or pulling out of a driveway to make sure there is no pedestrian or oncoming car. With experience, these precautions become so much a part of you that you do it instinctively. This applies to the application of all the information contained in this chapter. It is natural that when you are just learning the Moss Method of Self-analysis, you will not be able to put it all together. Your learning improves with months and years of experience. It's like learning to play the violin. You may be able to play a simple tune after a few weeks of practice, but as the time goes on your skill increases so that you will be able to play complicated music. Likewise with the Moss Method you will obtain some benefits almost right from the start, but it is the long range benefits that are important to strive for. I am a perfect example. In my forties and fifties I was a neurotic mess, with the beginning of organic breakdown. Today, only months away from my ninetieth birthday, I am free of all organic pathology, bounding with energy, in perfect physical and emotional health and enjoying life at its fullest. The latter are the long range benefits of making daily self-analysis a part of your life style.

The next and final chapter deals with the practical procedure of Step VI.

CHAPTER 16

STEP VII: ANALYTIC INTERPRETAtION
(Part Two)

Analytic interpretation with the Moss Method is based on traditional psychoanalytic principles. However, there are three significant differences between the Moss Method and traditional psychoanalytic procedures. These differences are an important aid in helping to overcome subjectivity, which the critics contend makes self-analysis unfeasible. What follows are those three differences.

First, the Moss Method assumes that the AGP syndrome exists in the unconscious of everyone. Thus you know what to search for right at the outset of your analytic session. Under the umbrella of the AGP syndrome, you will encounter all the traditional psychoanalytic phenomena and concepts: repression, fantasy constellation, sibling rivalry, sexuality, and all the other phenomena you learned in your analytic training.

Second, the Moss Method places emphasis on the search for the connection between 1) the dream, 2) the list, 3) the raw material collected in your notes. This concept does not exist in traditional psychoanalytic procedure.

Third, the application of Thought Provokers (TPs). The concept of bombardment of your unconscious resistance by the application of the four TPs does not exist in traditional psychoanalysis because it is a device originating with me.

The confluence of all the theoretical material in the previous chapters is the foundation upon which the analytic interpretation rests. The four Thought Provokers (TPs) listed in the previous chapter are:

TP#1 Reviewing Your Notes (all or part)

TP#2 Recall (past experiences)

TP#3 Questions Directed to Yourself

TP#4 Critical Scrutinization

TP#1 was discussed in the previous chapter. The remaining TPs will be discussed in this chapter.

TP #2 RECALL OF PAST EXPERIENCES. What now follows is a discussion of the concept of recall of memories as it pertains to the Moss Method of Self-analysis. I shall then describe the practical procedure of how this is done. A forgotten trauma is called an ANTECEDENT.[83] In all traumatic experience during subsequent periods of your life, antecedents may be activated. Because of the emotional charge originating from the antecedent, you often overreact to people, events, situations or to any item on your list in step 11. The rationale for recall of traumatic experiences is based on the premise that all the items on your list evoke an emotional response. (If it does not, it should not be on your list.) Since the residue of any emotional trauma is forever etched on your unconscious, it is reasonable to assume that each of the

---

83 Many cases of nervous breakdowns and even suicides have been reported by irresponsible and faulty hypnosis.

items on your list draws a charge of emotional energy from an unconscious residue of some past experience. Therefore, the emotional impact of an ongoing situation, such as the items on your list in step 11, cannot be determined only by your overt reality but also by a charge from an unconscious past trauma. Discovering the antecedent and relating it to an item on your list usually results in insight relative to your overreaction to that item. Why this occurs will be explained later on.

The Moss Method distinguishes between three kinds of forgotten memories:

A) TRIVIAL: These seem to be insignificant and of no consequence. Examples are: the name of a teacher in grammar school; yours or your friend's sixth-year birthday party, a trip to an amusement park or circus at age seven; your first piano lessen at age nine; a favorite fairy tale, a childhood melody, something your mother told you at age eleven, and thousands of other memories. Freud called this type of memory, SCREEN MEMORY.[84] By that he meant that there may be several different experiences that fit under the umbrella of the screen memory. Because of the umbrella-like character of screen memories, they are important. They may open up a new avenue of associations that may lead to a forgotten traumatic experience

B) TRAUMATIC: There is unconscious resistance to recall traumatic experiences because of the pain when opening up a wound. Some people would recommend dealing with such experiences by applying the metaphor, "Let sleeping dogs lie." However, until the experience is recalled and dealt with as an adult, it is the child's perception of the experience that remains unchanged even at the age of fifty or over. Childhood traumas may have a lifelong impact on your perceptions and behavior. Although

---

84 Horney, Karen; *Self-Analysis*; W.W. Norton; New York, NY, 1987, p. 158.

recalling a traumatic experience may be accompanied by pain and distress, there is absolutely NO HAZARD INVOLVED with self-analysis. Harm may result with dyadic analysis when recall is forced on a patient by faulty treatment or by hypnotic suggestion[85] In self-analysis, nothing can be recalled unless a state of readiness exists for that particular recall. The latter occurs only when your ego is strong enough to cope with the memory and when enough resistance has been removed for the experience to be recalled.[86]

By the time you reach adolescence, you have already experienced almost every conceivable negative emotional state.(fear, terror, panic, hysteria, frustration, envy, hostility, jealousy, etc.) many times over and over. A few of the many examples of childhood trauma are sexual abuse by an adult (very often incestuous), surgical, hospital or dental experience, the first day in school, any accident[87], separation from your mother and getting lost (at a shopping mall or in a subway station), severe punishment by parent or teacher for masturbating, a young child witnessing sexual intercourse of its parents and not comprehending what is happening. A trauma occurring during adult life, such as rape or witnessing carnage on a battlefield during war, may also be repressed from memory but is more accessible than a childhood trauma

C) ICR (Impossible to Cope with Reality:[88] These are memories of something ongoing in the H&N. Situations, events, conflicts that are impossible to cope with would result in a breakdown of

---

85 In Chapter 2, I described how under hypnosis a 45 year old physician relived a trauma that occurred at age three and a half.

86 The ICR phenomenon was discussed in Chapters 1 and 4.

87 Nothing emerges into consciousness accidentally. It is always provoked by an internal or external stimulus. See Chapter 13 dealing with free association.

88 t is a question that you, the psychoanalyst, should ask your patient.

function if nature did not come to the rescue to "keep the show on the road." By the phenomenon of REGRESSION, your reality is converted to one that you can cope with. That which you could not cope with is now in your unconscious, i.e., it is swept under the rug and forgotten. In Chapter 4, I discussed the cases of Little Joey, Sailor Jones and Aunt Margie. Each experienced an ICR phenomenon. Other examples of ICRs related to the H&N are: terminating a bad relationship or marriage, putting your objecting parent in a nursing home, needing to move to a different part of the country for health reasons, unemployment, oppressive guilt of a sexual nature. Usually a conversion symptom replaces the repressed reality. Little Joey developed thumb sucking, Sailor Jones a tic, and Aunt Margie a stutter.

Treatment of neurotic symptoms with the psychoanalytic modality necessitates recovery of the repressed reality, i.e., recall of that which caused the ICR. This produces spontaneous insight. The memory of what was repressed converts an ICR into a DCR (Difficult-to-Cope-with Reality) The symptom is no longer needed and it goes away. The ICR is often experienced symbolically in the manifest content of your dream.

Generally speaking, most people never make an effort to recall memories either trivial or traumatic. When recall does occur, it is always an unconscious, involuntary phenomenon, devoid of effort. It results from something ongoing which unconsciously provokes the memory.[89] Without analytic insight, an individual never connects the recalled trauma with the ongoing situation or event that brought about the recall. In contrast, the kind of recall sought for is the result of a concerted effort at recall. This effort may be a new experience for most people, one that they may have never had in their entire lives. But for you,

---

89 For details of the of each of the items on both lists, refer to Chapter 12.

my professional colleagues, it should not be a new experience if your training analysis was successful.

The following is a summary of the reasons for TP #2, RECALL:

1) Elimination for the need of defenses. The latter are necessary to keep repressed emotions and experiences from reaching consciousness. Sometimes a connectaion is made between the recalled antecedent (forgtten trauma) and an item on the list in step 11 that results in immediate insight.

2) Surge of energy. Repression of a traumatic experience consumes energy the same way as holding an inflated balloon under water does. Recall releases energy formerly consumed in maintaining defenses.

3) Recall gives you the opportunity to reevaluate past trauma from the vantage point of an adult instead of a child. Without recall the emotions involved in a repressed childhood trauma remains the same throughout adult life. Thus, without recall, you the adult, still have the same emotions relating to a repressed trauma that you had when you were in your childhood. But when it is recalled, it often seems trivial when examined from the vantage point of an adult.

TP#3 QUESTIONS DIRECTED TO YOURSELF. They fall into two categories. A) those of a general nature, B) those that deal specifically with the AGP syndrome.

A) General questions: The questions you ask yourself are based on the assumption that there is an overreaction or irrational attitude about an item on your list. The rationale for this assumption is that every conscious emotional reaction always arouses a concomitant unconscious response. Since you do not know what the latter is, the questions are designed to discover the response and its the connection to an item on your list. With the latter in mind, and while directing your attention to your list, you ask yourself the following questions: "What is going on in my life that I am not coming to grips with?...What is right under my nose, yet I can't see it?...What is it that I am afraid of?...What's causing me to overreact to this?" While asking yourself these questions—or any similar questions of your own choosing—you direct your attention to any one or combination of the items on the list. With some item on your list, you may unknowingly be making a mountain out of a molehill, a common occurrence of the unconscious. Examples are a letter from the IRS, or a summons for a traffic violation, a medical report of a biopsy, a letter from your stock broker, etc. These questions are provoking a response from your unconscious. It is important to record in your notebook whatever associations come to your mind.

The above questions were directed to yourself, the adult. You now direct questions to your child-self. The premise of these questions is based on the fact that your adult-self is superimposed on your child-self. YOU WILL NEVER CEASE BEING THE INFANT/CHILD YOU ONCE WERE! That is why as an adult when under stress or in a traumatic situation, you often behave irrationally, like a frightened child. With this in mind continue with, "What is it that I, a child of three (four, five, or six), am seeing and feeling that upsets me so much?...What am I afraid of...What gives me so much anxiety...what is threatening me..." Then select any item on the list and ask yourself, "How do I, the child of three, perceive this?...What am afraid of?..."

The success of these 'childish' questions depends on the degree to which you feel like the child you were and still continue to be. It is necessary to get down to the child level to whom these questions are directed. Don't feel silly or ashamed. Do it! The DAs (direct associations) that result from these questions are extremely important, albeit most DAs are still in symbolic form.

Although the answers don't emerge at this time, they provoke an unconscious response, Direct Associations (DAs). Continue to record into your notebook whatever new DAs come to mind, as you did during the previous steps. After recording your new DAs, directing your attention to them, you ask yourself, "Why do these thoughts come to me at this very moment?" The latter is a CARDINAL question that should be asked with all new associations. There may be hundreds of thoughts available to you, so ask, "Why is it this one?"[90] The associations to this question may lead directly to repressed material that up to now evaded cognizance although they are not yet recognizable because they are still is in symbolic form. There always is a connection between the new DAs and the item(s) on the Step ll list. Which item(s) you fix your attention on is not an accident or coincidence. It is determined by your unconscious.

B) *AGP Syndrome Questions*: You must be thoroughly familiar with the concept of the AGP syndrome discussed in Chapter 9 before proceeding with what follows. You direct your attention to your list in order to relate each item with one of the three components of the AGP syndrome. The presumption is that each item on your list has an AGP component. To illustrate this concept, I reproduce the two lists presented in Chapter 12. The first is the hypothetical one relating to myself.[91] The second is the list related to the case of MB, the CEO. (I suggest that you refresh your memory by reviewing Chapter 12 because knowing the details is imperative to grasping the concept that I describe.)

List #1[92]

1) dream

2) writing this book (*aggression*—creativity, replace father)

---

90 I've excluded items that deal with names relating to countertransference.

91 I am semi-retired as a therapist.

92 A musician friend of mine, a concert pianist, who knew the French composer Maurice Ravel, told me that Ravel would sometimes have an orgasm while composing. I believed my friend because he also told me that when he(my friend) played some compositions of Ravel, he would sometimes be sexually aroused.

3) Joan *(aggression-guilt)*
4) eat *(punishment—self-abuse)*
5) sex *(punishment—sexual failure)*
6) Ethel *(guilt)*—sibling rivalry)

List #2
1 dream
2 argument *(aggression)*
3 keys *(punishment—problems due to loss of keys)*
4 eat. *(punishment—self-abuse by overeating)*

Since each item on your list, except the dream, involves some degree of emotional distress, it is presumed that one of the three AGP components is always involved with each item. And because one component *can never* exist without the other two, simple POW logic dictates that the other two components are present in your unconscious. Thus, you have a road map of what to look for in your unconscious. The questions you direct to yourself are an attempt to discover and confront the other two. It usually is something in your H&N which you are repressing. Although you are oblivious of what it is, it may be the root cause of your anxiety or distress for that particular item on your list. The foregoing will be demonstrated in the *first* of the two lists, my own.

After the dream, the second item on my list is WRITING. Actually, this item has been on every list since I started writing this book. I consider this book an important project to which I have given top priority over all other activities. It has consumed a major portion of my time and energy.[93] Worthy and commendable as this writing project may be, my unconscious perceives

---

93 You must never forget that the unconscious is irrational. It also has the magical power of making a mountain out of a mole hill.

this project as a highly aggressive act.—This is also true of many creative writers, artists and others.—

On the first list above, alongside the cue word, "writing" is the word aggression, shown in underlined script. That is because writing this book provokes unconscious fantasies such as...1) creation; (there are many concepts in this book that are new and creative that never appeared in the literature); 2) a sexual act (many acts of creation are invested with some degree of sexuality.[94] 3) teacher (a father figure replacing my own father (Oedipal concept, with all its ramifications), and 4) sibling rivalry (my relationship with my colleagues is perceived as a family relationship in which I am attempting to outshine and show my superiority over my rival brothers and sisters, i.e., my professional colleagues.)[95]

Because my unconscious perceives writing this book as a highly aggressive act, I am certain that guilt is present in my unconscious. (based on the POW logic) But because it is repressed, I do not feel any guilt until I confront it during my self-analysis sessions. To prevent this guilt from impacting on my thoughts

---

94 Dr Pauline Clance described the feeling of being a fraud in her book, *The Impostor Phenomenon*, Bantam Books, 1989. It exists in many people high up the ladder of success. The more accolades one receives, the more one feels like a fraud. I have found this feeling in some of my colleagues I have had as patients.

95 Because many of the terms and concepts found in this book are based on the Moss Method, which is my own creation, I also had to devise a suitable vocabulary. Therefore, this glossary is unique in that it consists of many words and phrases that may not be found in the professional literature, or if found their usage in this book may have dissimilar meanings. Thus for one who has not read this book some definitions may appear unintelligible or confusing. This glossary may be used either for a dictionary of words and concepts or for review purpose during and after reading this book.

and behavior, especially regarding writing this book, I must deal with the fantasies described in the previous paragraph. I must feel the guilt on a gut level to cancel out its effects.

The following are some of the ways in which my guilt may impact on my actual life: the days that I have a successful self-analytic session, my ideas flow freely, as from a fountain. I am bounding with energy with an optimistic feeling about the outcome of my book. This animated feeling spreads over all other areas of my life, including my sexuality, notwithstanding the fact of my age. In contrast, when I skip my analytic sessions for several days, thereby not confronting my unconscious fantasies, I am less productive and often frustrated. My energetic drive shifts away from my writing to other interests and activities that I had put on the back burner in order to give priority to my writing. Such activities are music, (I am a violinist), reading, movies, sports, political activities (I am an activist), social activities, etc. divert me from writing. Although the latter are exciting and gratifying, they are diversions away from completing this book. I feel a sense of frustration which I perceive as punishment. (represented by underlined italics after items numbers 4 and 5 on the first list above). Both items cause me distress; overeating is self-abuse; sexual failure is painfully frustrating. Sometimes, I even feel like a fraud. *Who among you, my colleagues, do not at times feel like a fraud?*[96] *Self-analysis is the remedy that will overcome that feeling.*

With the foregoing as a model, return to your own list and do the same, i.e., after each item on the list place the AGP component involved with that item. After you have identified each of the

---

96 In chapter V, which dealt with the phenomenon of fantasy constel-lation, I discussed how parents identify with their own parents and treat their child as though it were their own childhood selves.

items on your list with the respective component of the AGP syndrome, you then apply the simple POW logic, described in the previous chapter. You select the item on your list that disturbs you the most. The questions you ask yourself are determined by which of the three components are involved. If the component is aggression, you know there is guilt. You ask yourself, "Why does this make me feel guilty?" This question is addressed to your child-self, who perceives the item from an entirely different point of view than you, the adult, perceive the item. You are trying to get at the cause of your irrational overreaction to the item. You try to discover why you are overreacting. Keep repeating the question. The associations that emerge are usually the reason for the overreaction, but in unrecognizable symbolic form. However, whatever emerges as a response to your questions should always be entered into your notebook, followed by the cardinal question, "Why do these thoughts occur to me at this time?" Sometimes you may recall an actual memory connected with the item, which results in instant insight. But most often the recall is in unrecognizable symbolism.

If the component to the item you selected is punishment, you ask your child-self, "For what am I being punished?...What have I done wrong...What do I feel guilty about...?" while directing your attention to your dream and the last associations entered in your notebook. These questions may result in the recall of an altercation you had with your mother, son, employer, neighbor or teacher. or an unpleasant sexual incident with your spouse or lover. (A sexual experience, good or bad, stirs up a variety of fantasies involving all of the three components.)The questions dealing with punishment may also evoke an antecedent that intensifies the heightened emotional charge for that item. Recall of an antecedent sometimes results in immediate insight.

However, the insight is usually in symbolic disguise, but not always.

You then select another item on your list and do the same. You always must ask your child-self, "What is the connection between 'this' item and 'that' item?" (selected by you) The items you select are never an accident. All the material that emerges during the questioning should be entered into your notebook for critical scrutinization.

TP#4 CRITICAL SCRUTINIZATION: From now on, analytic interpretation begins to occur. Seated at you desk, you must scrutinize the sequence of the your last emerging thoughts. You ask yourself, "What is the meaning of this chain of thoughts?" You then select an item on your list asking, "How is this chain of thoughts connected to the item?" You might suddenly remember that you did not mail your wife the monthly alimony check. This might be the molehill that became a mountain. It is significant that it was not even on your list. To recall that item may be the key that often leads directly to the cause of the distress in one or more items on your list. Record that item and continue the process of scanning your notes, especially the last entry, your dream and back to the list of Step 11, always searching for connections between them. Trivial and seemingly unrelated associations may emerge, such as mailing a letter, paying a bill, making a phone call, forgetting to call your sick mother who is in a nursing home, the argument you had with you son, etc. A new facet of something on the list may suddenly emerge. Whatever it is should be examined in the light of the sequence of last associations. This might be related to and connected with another item on the list. It could be anything that up to this point eluded you. The questions are constant bombardment of the unconscious mind. Cracks develop in the armor of your resistance. Emotional blocks tend to give way. New associations emerge, closer to pertinent material concealed in the unconscious, i.e., the ENEMY IN AMBUSH, the repressed material.

At this point you may remember to call the doctor for the results of the medical lab tests taken five days ago. You may have repressed the anxiety of the outcome of these tests. What may have occurred is that you forgot to put this important item on your list. You are in a state of denial so that you don't even feel the fear and anxiety regarding the outcome of the tests, or you may suddenly remember the frustration of last night's sexual fiasco. It could be any of a number of things that are too painful to cope with. Step VI strives to recall these things and to feel the intolerable emotions, i.e., to bring them back into awareness, to undo the state of denial. If you have no experience with the phenomenon of bombardment of the unconscious, you might be skeptical of the foregoing. But I assure you that it is very effective

You must never forget that everything that emerges into consciousness is NEVER an accident. It is always provoked by an internal or external stimulus. If recall of a memory occurs, you must ask yourself, "What is the connection between the recall, the last chain of associations, the dream and the list?" or "Why does this memory come to me for the first time after ten, twenty or thirty years?" All questions have one objective, namely, to establish relevancy and to make a connection between your recall, the chain of associations, your list and your dream. Very often the connection will give immediate analytic understanding why the overreaction occurs with a given item on the list. It will be accompanied by an emotional and/or physical change. Your back and neck muscles will relax, and/or you will involuntarily experience a change in respiration accompanied by a deep sigh. Every experienced analyst has personally experienced this change and/or has observed it in his patients when insight occurs.

When you mix your dream, the list, your associations and any recalled memory, and then you mix all this with questions, you are like the baker putting together the ingredients of a recipe and baking a cake. Baking is the metaphor for your self-analysis and the cake is your insight. Don't worry that your interpretation might be wrong because whatever you interpret comes from within yourself and not from an analyst, as may be the case with a dyadic relationship. Don't rule out or dismiss any interpretation as having no relevancy. Everything that emerges is relevant. The goal of the analysis is to discover the relevancy. When the connection is discovered, the chain is welded. Insight occurs like a flash of lightning that lights up the landscape.

Having presented the foregoing, I now direct your attention to the following facts and/or phenomena:

1 During the analytic session, you may be more disturbed than at the start of the session. That is because you are upsetting the homeostasis, thereby allowing repressed material that is painful to emerge into consciousness.

2 Not all sessions are successful. Sometimes you end up frustrated, believing the session was a failure. In the subsequent sessions you often experience an important breakthrough, i.e., insight. The previous sessions were necessary in that they contributed to the breakdown of resistance.

3 Often, before a major breakthrough of insight (or the recovery of a repressed conflict or traumatic memory) there is an exacerbation of symptoms. Every experienced analyst is familiar with this troublesome phenomenon. It is sometimes used to discredit the entire analytic process. Your patient may use this as a reason to terminate treatment. You, also, may have an exacerbation of

symptoms as analysis progresses. Don't become discouraged. The unconscious resistance is always looking for reasons to quit.

4. Only one of the three components of the AGP syndrome is necessary to recover the other two. This is done by applying the POW logic, namely that you are certain that there are two others if you have one, because one component never exists by itself.

5. Often what is recovered during a session, may be forgotten and must again be recovered during a subsequent session. You may again have to discover today what you painfully discovered yesterday, last week or last year. Sometimes you must recover the same material more than once, even during the same session, like learning again what you memorized and knew well just ten minutes ago (a name, a phone number out of the directory, an address, the spelling of a word you just looked up in the dictionary, etc.). This should not discourage you since it is a normal phenomenon.

Summary of Step Vl: The purpose of the last step is to achieve insight through analytic interpretation. You must be on the offensive in your search for interpretation and insight. You are continuously bombarding your unconscious defenses thereby lowering your resistance. During this step, you employ your intellect to its maximum capacity. Directing your attention to the most recent associations you must always ask yourself the cardinal question, "Why do these thoughts come to me at this time?" You must search for the AGP syndrome. You try to bring everything together (dream, list, raw material, past traumas) in order to form a welded chain, i.e., to achieve insight.

When should one terminate one's analytic session? There are several factors that determine this: 1) When the time allotted for any given session comes to an end, i.e., from 45 to 60 minutes.— During periods of emotional crisis. or when a distressing conflict exists, it is advisable to increase the time to as much as two hours or more.—

2) When you has gained insight, i.e., the connection between any of the items on the list of Step 11 with what previously was concealed in your unconscious.—This does not happen at every session. Perhaps during the same day, while you are with a patient, a flash of insight may suddenly emerge. At times nothing seems to happen for several session then insight bursts forth at a subsequent session. The previous sessions were not wasted. They were needed to overcome resistance—.

The following is a breakdown of the time for each of the six steps:

Step I (the dream)	2 to 4 minutes
Step 11 (the list)	2 to 3 minutes
Step 111 (DA)	5 to 10 minutes
Step IV (NDA.)	5 to 10 minutes
Step V (Recap.)	5 to 10 minutes
Step Vl (Analy. Interpret.)	30 minutes plus.

In round figures, the total time adds up to about 60 minutes. More time on one step necessitates less time on another. The above time schedule need not be adhered to rigidly. It is only a guide. Obviously, flexibility is essential. When you will have had sufficient experience with the Moss Method, you may modify the above time schedule. You will not have to spend so much time with each session. As you grow older, and *if* you continue the process of growth and maturity—not all people who grow old do—you will not need to be so disciplined in regards to regular daily sessions. You even may skip days or weeks. But you must never abandon self- analysis, because NO ONE IS EVER FREE OF CONFLICT. I am convinced that there is no better approach to dealing with conflict than self-analysis. Thus, you will avoid the risk of domination by an ENEMY IN AMBUSH concealed in your unconscious.

You must keep on the 'front burners' of your intellect the principles discussed in this book and other basics you've learned during your training as an analyst. With this formula you will overcome much of your subjectivity that many claim to be an obstacle to self-analysis. The success of self-analysis depends on your persistence, which in turn depends on your will and determination to make continued growth and maturity the number one priority of your life. I made this commitment to myself fifty years ago. Now, only months away from my ninety first birthday, I am happy to say that it paid off beyond expectations. It will do the same for you if you make the same commitment I did. The spin-off of this commitment is that you will become a far better analyst. You will achieve a greater satisfaction not only from your professional work but you will also derive the maximum fulfillment and happiness from life.

GLOSSARY[97]

AGGRESSION: Your unconscious perceives aggression quite differently from how your conscious mind does. What the conscious perceives as trivial may be unconsciously monumental. Aggression exists not only in our overt actions but also in our fantasies, such as in dreams. There are four categories as it relates to the AGP syndrome: 1)PARENTAL DEFIANCE 2) SEXUAL 3) BEHAVIORAL 4) EMOTIONAL EXPRESSION.

AGP SYNDROME: A homeostatic relationship between one's aggression, guilt and the punishment. It starts to form at birth. By the time one reaches the tender age of five, it already is well established. It remains as a vital force until death.

---

97 Because many of the terms and concepts found in this book are based on the Moss Method, which is my own creation, I also had to devise a suitable vocabulary. Therefore, this glossary is unique in that it consists of many words and phrases that may not be found in the professional literature, or if found their usage in this book may have dissimilar meanings. Thus for one who has not read this book some definitions may appear unintelligible or confusing. This glossary may be used either for a dictionary of words and concepts or for review purpose during and after reading this book.

ANTECEDENT: A past experience or period of one's life characterized by emotional trauma that leaves a residual emotional nidus in one's unconscious. This can become reactivated at some future time. (See NIDUS.)

ASSOCIATION: The term Free Association (FA)in the professional literature refers to those thoughts/ideas that emerge from the unconscious during the analytic process. This book describes two kinds of FAs, Directed Association (DA) and Non- directed Association (NDA).

1) DAs are the associations (thoughts) that emerge into consciousness when one directs his/her attention to an object such as the dream or any item on the list.

2) NDAs are the associations (thoughts) that emerge into consciousness when one's intellect is totally passive. In contrast to DAs, the intellect is passive, one does not think of anything nor directs his/her attention to anything. The mind is free wheeling.

AWARENESS: In the Moss Method it exists on two levels: 1) Focal awareness (central consciousness, cognizance). Intellectual cognizance of a thought arising from the preconscious (unconscious) and remaining long enough to be recorded in one's notes. 2) Peripheral awareness. A thought which does not achieve cognizance because it lies beyond the range of the focal center of one's awareness.

BREAKTHROUGH In Step Vl of the Moss Method, an association (or chain of associations) that produces awareness of a connection between the dream, the list, raw material in one's notebook, recalled memories and the exaggerated or irrational character of any of the items on the list is considered a penetration into the armor of one's unconscious resistance (see PAY DIRT.)

CATCH A CAT BY THE TAIL: The willful and disciplined intellectual process of retrieving a thought or train of thoughts (associations or chain of associations) that had flitted into focal consciousness but slipped back into the unconscious.

CENSORSHIP: The involuntary and uncontrollable mental process of blocking or preventing an emotion, thought or idea from emerging into consciousness.

CHAIN OF ASSOCIATIONS: Each association, or thought, that emerges into focal consciousness is the product of a previous thought. It in turn produces new thoughts/associations. Collectively the individual thoughts are linked together into a chain of associations. (See LINK in CHAIN of ASSOCIATIONS)

CONTROLLED STIMULUS: An intellectual device used to redirect one's chain of associations (train of thoughts) for the purpose of producing a change in the direction, contents or character of associations. (See THOUGHT PROVOKER.)

DEFENSE MECHANISM: A phenomenon that serves to keep that part of the unconscious with which an individual can not cope repressed from the conscious mind..

DIFFICULT to-COPE-with REALITY (DCR): By means of analyitic insight an IMPOSSIBLE to-COPE-with REALITY (ICR) reaches consciousness, i.e., the reality is no longer repressed. The conscious reality, even though it is no longer repressed, may be difficult to cope with.

DIRECT ASSOCIATION: (DA) (See ASSOCIATION.)

DISPLACEMENT: The unconscious, involuntary phenomenon of directing an intolerable emotion or drive away from its original source to another symbolically related object. It is nature's way of releasing psychic energy bottled up and concealed from consciousness. Repressed sexual energy is often displaced on to nonsexual situations, objects or individuals so that the sexual element remains disguised and unrecognizable.

DREAM, MANIFEST- LATENT: The MANIFEST content is that part of the dream that reaches the conscious mind disguised in sybolism. The LATENT content is the concealed part of the dream underlying its meaning.

EMOTIONAL ABSCESS: A nidus of emotionally repressed material located in the unconscious. It impacts on one's conscious thoughts, perception and behavior. It often results in aberrated, neurotic function, such as obsessions, phobias, compulsive behavior, paranoia and/or organic illness. The negative effects emanating from an emotional abscess may be considered PUS or POISON. Since one is not aware of the existence of the emotional abscess, it may be thought of as AN ENEMY IN AMBUSH. Any forgotten or repressed emotional trauma may leave an emotional abscess in its wake. (See ANTECEDENT, EMOTIONAL NIDUS, ENEMY IN AMBUSH and EMOTIONAL CHARGE.)

EMOTIONAL ANESTHESIA: Involunntary repression of painful emotions (ariising from rejection, bereavement, failure, emotions of guilt, sexual aggression, hostility, envy, jealousy, etc.) that cause unbearable suffering. It enables one to "keep the show on the road." (See REPRESSION, KEEP THE SHOW ON THE ROAD, and PSYCHIC ANESTHESIA.)

EMOTIONAL CHARGE: Energy that emanates from a forgotten trauma that is displaced on any of the items listed in Step II. (See DISPLACEMENT, ANTECEDENT.)

EMOTIONAL FIX: A state of self-suggestion (autosuggestion) that temporarily alters one's belief system. It is related to a cult, a fad, and sometimes to faulty psychotherapy and characterized by a temporary state of well-being, contentment and self-satisfaction. Ultimately the autosuggestion wears off and the individual is left with a feeling of disappointment, frustration and depression.

EMOTIONAL NIDUS (See NIDUS.): The source in one's unconscious from which 'Pus' or 'poison' originates resulting from a forgotten trauma. (See ENEMY IN AMBUSH.)

ENEMY IN AMBUSH Repressed material which impacts negatively on the conscious mind (behavior, perception). The individual is unaware of the havoc in one's life it may produce.

ENVIRONMENT, INNER and OUTER: (See UNIVERSE.)

FANTASY: An idea or image, or a series of such ideas or images, present in the mind but having no concrete or objective reality. (dictionary definition)

FANTASY CONSTELLATION: The type of fantasy in which one identifies with other individuals. There are two ARCHETYPES from which dozens of variations may be fabricated by unconscious identification 1) Child—Parent; 2) Child—Child. The character of interpersonal relationships is often determined by variations of the above two kinds of fantasy constellation

FLASH INSIGHT: Insight that appears suddenly. Although it lasts only for an instant, its effects generally linger for hours, days, weeks, or longer. (See INSIGHT.)

FRAGMENTATION (of a symbol) A symbol in the manifest content of dreams sometimes consists of several different parts. These separate parts must be joined and decoded to arrive at the disguised latent meaning of the dream. (See INVERSION.)

FREE ASSOCIATION (FA): (See ASSOCIATION.)

FUGITIVE FROM ONESELF: State of alienation resulting from the accumulation of 'forbidden' thoughts and/or emotions being repressed. (See DENIAL REACTION.)

HERE AND NOW (H&N): The current ongoing emotional problems, stresses, strains and conflicts distinct from those of the past (yesterday, last week, last year or 20 years ago). The list in Step II is derived from the H&N.

HOMEOSTASIS: The unconscious, balanced relationship between between guilt that results from one's aggression—as perceived by the unconscious—and the need for punishment. Development of homeostasis starts early in childhood as a consequence of the discipline imposed on the child by the parents and/or parent substitutes. It is fully developed in the postadolescent period of one's life, and it remains constant throughout life.

HUMANIZATION: Process by which individuals adopt animalistic instincts to live in a human society according to society's established mores. This necessitates repression of forbidden acts and/or thoughts. Conflict is the result of the collision between repressed material—experiences, conflicts and/or fantasies—and what is socially/culturally permissible.

IMPOSSIBE-to-COPE-with REALITY (ICR): A reality that produces guilt resulting from forbidden acts. The guilt is so intense that it creates a crisis with which the individual sometimes finds it impossible to cope. Repression of such reality enables the individual to continue to function. (See KEEP the SHOW on the ROAD.)

INSIGHT: Discovery of the connection between the items on the list in Step II and repressed material. Intellectual awareness of the connection, without the gut-level feeling, does not produce insight.

KEEP THE SHOW ON THE ROAD: To maintain function when faced with an ICR , one regresses to a period of life when such reality did not exist. Thus, the overt reality is repressed. (See ICR.)

LATENT CONTENT OF DREAM: (See DREAM.)

LINK in CHAIN of ASSOCIATIONS: The association, or thought, that emerges into consciousness was provoked by a previous thought, in turn resulting in the production of new associations or thoughts. Each individual association is, therefore, linked together as a chain.

MAKING A MOUNTAIN OUT OF A MOLE HILL: Magnification of what the conscious mind perceives as a small, trivial matter or concern (traffic violation, tax audit, etc.) until the unconscious perceives it as dangerous and a serious matter of mountainous proportion.

LATENT CONTENT OF DREAM: (See DREAM)

MIND RUNS DRY: Cessation of the flow of associations during steps lll, IV or V. The mind is blank.

NEGATIVE RATIONALIZATION: Denigration of an association and/or thought during any of the steps of the Moss Method because the belief or feeling that the given thought is trivial, insignificant or unimportant. It, therefore, is ignored and is not recorded into one's notes. Such rationalization stems from resistance. All thoughts and/ or associations during the analytic procedure are important and must be recorded.

NIDUS (emotional): An area in one's unconscious where emotions resulting from a forgotten trauma are lodged. It is from this source that emotional charges of psychic energy arise that are displaced on item(s) on the list in Step ll. (See EMOTIONAL ABSCESS, ANTECEDENT.)

OBSESSION: Involuntary, unwanted compulsive behavior or thoughts.

OMNISEXANT: Relating to the unconscious fantasies of a child about the adult's power of sexual gratification with any person, in whatever manner conceivable. This is based on the fact that the child perceives the adult as omnipotent and omniscient.

OUTCROPPING: The emergence of thoughts/associations from the unconscious into consciousness.

PAY DIRT Insight achieved from making the connection between the last associations and the dream and/or the list and/or a forgotten memory. (See BREAKTHROUGH.)

PERIPHERAL AWARENESS: (See AWARENESS.)

PSYCHIC ANESTHESIA: Repression of emotional pain that is too difficult to cope with (rejection, bereavement, frustrating failure, sexual aggression, hostility, envy, jealousy, etc.) (See DENIAL REACTION, ICR, REGRESSION and REPRESSION.)

PSYCHIC DYNAMO: The powerful source of pent-up sexual energy originating from the survival instinct.

PSYCHIC ENERGY: Energy expended on intellectual and emotional activities: thought processes, perception, fantasy, repression, displacement, etc. (See PSYCHIC DYNAMO.)

PUDDLE OF WATER (POW) The term applied to the logic that when one sees a puddle of water in the morning upon awakening, one could know with CERTAINTY that it rained during the night if there was no other way of that puddle of water to have gotten there unless it rained.

REGRESSION: An involuntary return of the psyche to a past period of one's life when current reality was nonexistent. (See ICR, REPRESSION and KEEP THE SHOW ON THE ROAD.)

REPORTING: Discussion at the start of a dyadic analytic session regarding the events that occurred since the last session. The material reported is the 'here and now.' In self-analysis it is analogous to the list in Step II.

REPRESSION: The involuntary phenomenon of erasing from consciousness material impossible to cope with (ICR), i.e., emotions, conflicts, memories, etc. What is repressed is stored in the unconscious. i.e., forgotten, swept under the rug. (See REGRESSION, ICR and Keep the Show on the Road.)

RESISTANCE: That phenomenon of the unconscious mind that is used as a defense against confrontation (awareness, cognizance) of that material with which it is impossible to cope (ICR). IT consists of defenses that impede the analytic process.

SCANNING Rapidly looking over one's notes in Step V and Step VI of the Moss Method in which the mind selects any item in the written notes. What one selects is not accidental. It is determined by the unconscious.

SCRUTINIZATION, CRITICAL: The procedure done in Step VI of the Moss Method using the fourth TP to arrive at and to understand the relevance and connection among the dream, the items on the list, the material in the notes and/or the most recent associations. Insight occurs when the connection is made.

SEXUAL POWERHOUSE: (See PSYCHIC DYNAMO.)

SEXUAL POWDER KEG Powerful, pent-up sexual energy resulting from cultural conditioning that invests the sexual drive with conditions and restrictions.

STATE OF READINESS: Sufficiently lowered resistance, as a result of the analytic process, allows repressed material to emerge into consciousness in recognizable form. The level of resistance always determines which thoughts (associations) emerge into consciousness.

SUFFERING, PRIMARY and SECONDARY: PRIMARY SUFFERING results directly from a traumatically painful reality. However, if the reality becomes an ICR (impossible-to cope-with reality), one involuntarily regresses and thereby represses the ICR and all the painful emotions related to the ICR. The consequence of this, i.e., the avoidance of pain, results in the displacement of the repressed material to areas that produce irrational/aberratant behavior and/or neurotic symptoms. The resulting suffering is known as SECONDARY SUFFERING. There never is a conscious connection between the secondary suffering and the repressed ICR, except by means of the analytic process.

SURVIVAL INSTINCT: The strongest force of all life. There are two separate survival instincts: 1) survival of the species and 2) survival of the organism. Each is intertwined with the other. Survival of the species could not occur unless the individual organism survives long enough to fulfill its reproductive purpose. In the human animal the survival of the species instinct is the sexual drive.

SURVIVAL EQUATION: To the infant and to the growing child, who are dependent for survival on their parents (or parent substitutes), love and acceptance is EQUATED to security and well-being.

SWEEP UNDER THE RUG Involuntary repression from the consciousness of those painful conflicts in which one is dead-locked and unable to find a resolution, or of emotions that one finds impossible to cope with (ICR). (See ICR, REPRESSION and REGRESSION.)

SYMBOLISM: A form of unconsciously codified thoughts, ideas, emotions, things, people, reality, or parts of one's anatomy, made unrecognizable to the conscious intellect. The disguised language can be decoded, understood and/or interpreted, only through the analytic process. (See FRAGMENTATION of a SYMBOL and MANIFEST CONTENT of DREAMS.)

TAILGATE: In the analytic process there are times that a series of thoughts (associations) emerges into focal consciousness in such rapid succession that it is impossible to capture and/or record all of them. Because only one association can be recorded (written in one's notes) at any given moment, the other associations are backed up, bumper to bumper, as a line of cars in a traffic jam, waiting their turn to be recorded.

THOUGHT PROVOKER (TP): The devices used to stimulate additional associations in Steps V and Step VI of the Moss Method of Self-analysis. There are four kinds: 1) rereading one's notes; 2) recall of past memories, 3) questions directed to oneself, and 4) critical scrutinization.

TRIVIALIZATION: The tendency to rationalize thoughts or associations during the analytic procedure as trivial, irrelevant or unimportant. It is a manifestation of resistance.

UNCONSCIOUS: The sum total of all mental processes occurring under the level of awareness. Synonyms in this text are inner universe, inner environment, preconscious and peripheral consciousness. (See INNER and OUTER UNIVERSE.)

UNIVERSE, INNER and OUTER: Everything that exists inside of one's unconscious is considered the inner universe (inner environment). In contrast everything that exists outside the realm of one's unconscious is considered the outer universe (outer environment). In the Moss Method, the conscious mind is considered part of the outer universe and the unconscious mind as the inner universe.

WELDED CHAIN OF ASSOCIATIONS: During the analytic process, the individual thoughts or associations that emerge into consciousness are considered links in the chain of associations. Connecting the individual links results in a welded chain of associations and produces insight. (See ASSOCIATION, CHAIN OF ASSOCIATION.)

WHAT and HOW: The WHAT is the AGP and other material to search for in the last step of The Moss Method. The HOW is the actual procedure of carrying out the search.

ZERO IN: During scanning one's notes in Steps V and VI, the unconscious will involuntarily cause the intellect to select that with which it is ready to deal. The readiness results from lowered resistance. The process of selectivity is known as zeroing in. The unconscious will overlook that with which it is not yet ready to deal.